ON EDUCATION

THE FUTURE IN EDUCATION
AND
EDUCATION FOR A WORLD ADRIFT

BY

SIR RICHARD LIVINGSTONE

Sometime President of
Corpus Christi College, Oxford

CAMBRIDGE
AT THE UNIVERSITY PRESS
1954

CAMBRIDGE UNIVERSITY PRESS
Cambridge, New York, Melbourne, Madrid, Cape Town,
Singapore, São Paulo, Delhi, Mexico City

Cambridge University Press
The Edinburgh Building, Cambridge CB2 8RU, UK

Published in the United States of America by Cambridge University Press, New York

www.cambridge.org
Information on this title: www.cambridge.org/9781107622098

First published separately
'The Future in Education' 1941
'Education for a World Adrift' 1943
Published in U.S.A as 'On Education' 1944
Published in U.K. as 'On Education' 1954

Translations
'The Future in Education': German,
Italian, Arabic, Polish, Danish, Greek
'Education for a World Adrift': German,
Italian, Polish
First published 1954
First paperback edition 2013

A catalogue record for this publication is available from the British Library

ISBN 978-1-107-62209-8 Paperback

CONTENTS

Preface to this edition   *page* ix

THE FUTURE IN EDUCATION

Preface to the first edition   3

I   The Educational Problem   7

The achievement and the failure of our educational system, p. 7:
Most of the population withdrawn from all education at 15: this
an absurdity and a disaster, p. 8

II   An Ignored Educational Principle   12

A vital principle of education, p. 12: Aristotle on the unfitness of the
young for political or philosophical study, p. 13: Newman on two
kinds of apprehension, p. 14: Illumination of literature by experience
illustrated from Thucydides, Tacitus, Shakespeare, p. 17: Chesterfield
on cross-fertilisation of theory and experience, p. 20: Application of
this to education, p. 21: The value and limitations of the study of
history, politics and kindred subjects at school and university,
p. 22: Inert ideas in education, p. 31

III   The Way Out   33

How is the mass of the population to be educated? Inadequacy of
raising the school-age or of 'secondary education for all', p. 33:
The way out lies through part-time continued education followed
by Adult Education, p. 37: Capacity for intellectual and artistic
interests widespread; this illustrated by recent developments, p. 39:
The model of the Danish People's High Schools, p. 41: Their three
secrets; they are (*a*) for adults, (*b*) residential and social institutions,
(*c*) inspired by spiritual ideals, p. 44: Their influence on Danish
agriculture and politics, p. 52: Can their system be adapted to our
conditions? p. 54: How Adult Education might develop here, p. 57

IV   Cultural Studies in Adult Education   *page* 59

Liberal education defined, p. 59: Scientific and Humanist elements
in it, p. 63: Problem of interesting the average man in history and
literature; history as treated in the Danish P.H.S. and in the Bible,
p. 65: Literature as (*a*) enlargement of experience, (*b*) interpretation
of life, p. 69: Adult Education and our spiritual chaos, p. 74

V   Adult Education for the Educated   76

The absurdity of ceasing systematic education on leaving school or
university, p. 76: Bad effects of our present practice, p. 78: How to
keep the middle-aged young, p. 80: Need to study religion, morals
and politics in later life, p. 81: Is Adult Education for the educated
practicable? Recent experiments in it, p. 83: The part to be played
in it by (*a*) the Universities, (*b*) the State and Public Bodies, p. 85:
Value of such study to the Social Sciences; Nuffield College, p. 88

Postscript. Secondary Education: 92
   A Criticism

Moral and intellectual chaos of Western Civilisation, p. 92: Due
to the weakening of Christianity and Hellenism, the two influences
from which it draws its spiritual life, p. 94: How can education
help? Its present chaos and need of co-ordination, p. 95: Importance
in education of distinguishing Means and Ends, p. 97: Literature
and history as sources of Ends, p. 100: Philosophy of life to be derived
from study of Greek thought and of Christianity, p. 102

EDUCATION FOR A WORLD ADRIFT

Preface to the first edition   109

I   The Problem   115

An age of change, p. 115: Its double problem, material and spiritual,
p. 118: Democracy may not help us, p. 120: Lack of standards in the
pre-war world, p. 121: Our double revolution, political and spiritual,
p. 126: The weakening of spiritual influences by the spirit of criticism;
contrast between the Victorian and post-Victorian ages, p. 127:
A balance-sheet, p. 131: Need of the 'science of good and evil', p. 133

II Character and its Training page 135

The virtues and defects of our education, p. 135: Its failure to impart values and its unconscious utilitarianism, p. 137: Inadequate suggestions for integrating it, p. 141: The residential school—its success and failure in training character, p. 143: The triple task of education, p. 148: Importance of its spiritual side, p. 149: Need of a vision of the first-rate, p. 151

III The Training of Character through History and Literature 156

Education as spiritual training, p. 156: Use of history for this purpose, p. 158: Triple strand in progress—political, scientific, spiritual, p. 159: Different types in spiritual life, p. 162: Use of literature, p. 163: Corrupting influences in history and literature, p. 168: Necessity of moral judgements in history, p. 172: Moral judgements in literature; objections to expurgation; Fitzgerald and Housman, p. 173

IV From Atmosphere to Reason 182

Plato on early education as a training in right habits, p. 182: Need of a definite philosophy; but what philosophy? p. 183: Common elements in the spiritual life of Western civilisation; Greek thought and Christianity creators of the soul of our civilisation, p. 184: Greek thought as an introduction to natural religion and morals; the ideal of 'virtue', p. 186: Religious education; the teaching of Christianity, p. 193: W. Lippmann on the weakness in modern education, p. 196: Danger of 'tyrannising' over the mind, p. 198

V Two Dragons in the Road 203

Hindrances to education; (a) bad effect of examinations on teacher and pupil, p. 203; and on the curriculum, p. 205: Their importance tends to increase; essential to diminish it, p. 207: (b) bad effect of specialisation, p. 209: Dewey criticised, p. 211: The remedy, p. 212

VI Education for Citizenship 214

Greece the mother of education for citizenship; our neglect of it, p. 214: Citizenship defined; need for training in it, p. 217: Three elements in such training: (a) 'civics'; its limitations; need for it at the adult stage, p. 218: (b) a vision of the ideal; Thucydides on patriotism, Plato on the State as a family, p. 223: (c) citizenship learnt by living as a citizen; education in it given to the British by religion, history and other agencies, p. 226: The influence of the residential school, p. 228: The nursery school, day school and newer universities, p. 229: Future provision for training in citizenship, p. 231

PREFACE TO THIS EDITION

This volume contains two books which were originally published separately. A few minor changes have been made to bring statistics, etc. up-to-date.

Education for a World Adrift is an attempt to consider what education can do to remedy the lack of standards and clear beliefs which is the most dangerous weakness of the Western world. *The Future in Education* was the fruit of reflection on the results of our present educational system. We might with advantage more often consider how far it misses or achieves its aims. As it is, we are like doctors who administer doses from a number of stock medicines but never ask what effect they have on the health of their patients. The treatment is reasonably successful with a small minority, but the rest leave our surgeries with no desire to take any more of the medicines which we think indispensable to their health, and often with a strong aversion to them. The real benefit of school life—and it is a great benefit—is its effect on the character, the result of living an ordered life under discipline and in good conditions. But the other aims for which schools are supposed to exist are very imperfectly attained by most of their pupils. It is not a question of what the ordinary boy or girl knows or does not know, when they leave school; it is a question of the interests and tastes which they carry with them into life. Here our education fails. If anyone thinks this too pessimistic a view, let him consider the cheaper London newspapers and the average film, which presumably reflect the tastes of the ordinary citizen; let him note the appeal of 'the comics'; let him observe what passengers in trains are reading, and ask what percentage of the population ever read anything worth while; let him listen to the complaints of the Workers' Educational Association that the number of those working men who wish to attend their classes is diminishing. We have got a political democracy, but not yet an educated one. That is our problem. It cannot be solved without adult education.

The public as a whole does not yet realise this. It regards education as something for childhood and adolescence and perhaps for a few years more, and fancies that all will be well if we extend and improve our school system. That no doubt is desirable, but the example of America where the school leaving-age is 16 and often 18, and where some two and a half millions attend College, shows that such remedies do not cure the disease; for, to put it mildly, the American nation is not better educated than our own.

But the tide is slowly changing. Perhaps the most striking educational development in Britain since the war is the foundation of more than twenty Residential Colleges for Adult Education, most of them sponsored by Local Education Authorities, some by universities, some by bodies like the Y.M.C.A. and the Women's Institutes, one or two by private enterprise. In view of the difficulties of finance and building, this is remarkable. And outside the residential field, there is the much larger volume of work carried on by voluntary bodies, and by Local Education Authorities under the provisions for 'Further Education' in the Butler Act. Though there is far to go and progress is slow, we are moving on the road which leads to an educated democracy.

R. W. LIVINGSTONE

4 June 1953

THE
FUTURE IN EDUCATION

PREFACE TO THE FIRST EDITION

This book does not deal with primary, technical, university, nor, except for an isolated chapter, with secondary, education. All these, though susceptible of development and improvement, are firmly established. The great need and opportunity is in another field, of which a corner has been occupied but of which much is barely cultivated and part unexplored. The pressing problem is to give the masses of the nation some higher education, which will include that study of human ideals and achievement which we call literature, history and politics, and that study of the material universe which we call science. In some form, these are essential to the full development of all human beings, but at present the majority of the nation has no chance of studying them. How can this be altered? That, the most serious educational problem of the day, is the main subject of this book, which does not attempt to deal with details of organisation, but rather to suggest the principles to be followed.

I am convinced that secondary or post-primary education can give little help in solving the problem and that it can only be solved by adult education. Nothing is more needed than to revise our views as to the best age for 'cultural' education. If we could do that, the road would be open for one of the great educational advances of history. Ask anyone what is the right age for education, and the reply will probably be 'from 6 to 15 or 16, with an extension to 18 for more intelligent children, and to 21 or 22 for a picked few'. I do not of course question the need for elementary education to 14 or 15, the uses of secondary and university education for some, and the importance for

3   I-2

all of maintaining between 14 and 18 some contact with educational influences. But, after 50 years spent in receiving or giving education, I am convinced that for the studies in question the years after 18 are a better age, and those after 30 better still.

This may seem a paradox. But everyone witnesses to its truth who says 'I wish I could have my education again'; and who, at some time of his life, has not said it? That phrase is the best argument for my view. Expanded, it would read: 'I was educated at an age when I knew so little of life that I could not really understand the meaning or use of education. Now that I have seen something of the world and of human beings, I realise what education can do for me and the real value and significance of many subjects which I studied years ago with little appetite and less understanding under the compulsion of a teacher or an examination. If I could only go back and have again the chances which I wasted, simply because I was not old enough to use them!'

In Chapter II I have given my view of the reasons why we all wish to have our education again, and I do not believe that there is any answer to the arguments there. Roughly my contention is that for full appreciation and the most fruitful study of the subjects in question—history, literature, and politics—experience of life is necessary. If so, certain conclusions follow.

First: the years of post-primary education (i.e. from 15 to 18) cannot be the best period for these studies. In particular the ordinary man of average or low intellectual ability will get little from them before the age of 18; and therefore the majority (who at present receive no education after the age of 14) can only study them satisfactorily in their adult years.

Second: without an extended system of adult education

4

we cannot have an educated nation (suggestions for such a system are given in Chapters III and IV).

Third: those who receive a secondary education—graduates included—need an opportunity for resuming study methodically in later years when they have had experience of life (Chapter V).

The Postscript is unconnected with the main theme of the book and deals with a grave weakness in our secondary education, from whose effects, unless it is remedied, the nation will increasingly suffer.

The book develops ideas advanced in the Presidential Address to the Education Section of the British Association in 1934; part of Chapter II has appeared in the *Hibbert Journal* and most of Chapter V in *Public Administration*. Professor Ernest Barker and Sir Alfred Zimmern read the book in manuscript and helped me with valuable suggestions.

R. W. L.

March 1941

CHAPTER I

THE EDUCATIONAL PROBLEM

Why are we an uneducated nation and how can we become an educated one? We have compulsory education, magnificent schools, an impressive array of teachers, and an enormous educational budget. Yet most of the passengers in a railway carriage will be reading the *Daily Mirror*; and the *News of the World* has a circulation of between three and four millions. The advertisements, cheap newspapers and films of a country are the best index of what appeals to its masses. What view would posterity form of our civilisation from these manifestations of its taste and intelligence? Contrast with our cinema the drama which the whole Athenian people watched in the bright March weather millennia ago. What fraction of our masses would sit through a performance of the *Trilogy* or the *Philoctetes*?

It is not that education has been neglected. Between the Forster Education Act of 1870 and the 1891 Act the country organised elementary education. The Balfour Act of 1902 began a new era in the organisation of secondary education. In the early years of the twentieth century universities were created throughout the country. Since 1889 technical instruction has been developed thoroughly and effectively. That is a great achievement. In all these fields—university, secondary, technical, elementary—the problem has been faced and roughly solved. Improvements and developments will come; but the main lines have been well laid and are not likely to be altered. We have the tools, even if we may often use them ineffectively. In the future they may be improved and elaborated, but the chief improvement necessary is that we should learn more of their use and purpose, and our worst failures are due to the fact that we drift into and through education in a mechanical, automatic, unthinking way, instead of clearly defining to our own minds what we wish education to do for us and asking whether it is doing it and, if not, why not. Like religion, education quickly degenerates into a routine; then its meaning and its effects are lost. Still the late nineteenth and early twentieth centuries have done a great and solid work in it. So far, so good.

But all this still leaves a vast gap—I had almost said, a bottomless pit—in our national education. Some 70 per cent of the children of the nation are entirely withdrawn from any educational influence at the age of 15.[1] But education which ends at that age is not an education. It might be plausibly argued that nearly all the money spent on elementary education is wasted, because the system is, on the face of it, absurd. If you taught a child the letters of the alphabet and then stopped, you would probably consider that you had thrown time away in teaching him the ABC. Yet that is what we do in our elementary education. Elementary education is not complete in itself. It is preparatory. It prepares the pupil to go on to something else, and puts his foot on the first step of the ladder of knowledge. But in fact the vast majority go on to nothing else, they never climb higher on the ladder than the first step. How many pupils whose education ceases when they leave an elementary school maintain afterwards anything that can be called intellectual interest? How many think with any real seriousness about the problems of politics on which as electors they are expected to decide? How many

[1] In 1951–2, 178,634 boys left secondary modern and similar schools on reaching the age of fifteen to go into employment or for some other reason. Of these, 1,773 left for full-time education elsewhere.

8

read books worth reading? How many read books at all?[1]
What have they gained adequate to the vast sums spent on
them? The chief uses of our present elementary system are
to enable a minority to proceed to further education, and
the rest to read the cheap press. I am not criticising our
elementary schools or their teachers, or denying the necessity of elementary education for all. But unless it leads on
to something else, it is as useless as a ladder which has no
rungs beyond one or two at its bottom or as a railway from
Oxford to London which ends at Didcot. To cease education at 15 is as unnatural as to die at 15. The one is physical
death, the other intellectual death. In fact we have left
the vast majority of the population without any kind of
liberal education. We have provided for the minority who
attend secondary school and university. We have shown
the rest a glimpse of the promised land, and left them outside it. Aristotle may have gone too far when he said that
the object of education was to help men to use their leisure
rightly. But we have treated the majority as if they were to
have no leisure, or as if it did not matter how they used
what leisure they had. Art, music, science, literature were
for the few. The rest were disinherited from some of the
purest and highest pleasures. They might be machines or
animals; men in the full sense of the word they could not
be. That is the type of democracy with which we have been,
and are, content.

It mattered, perhaps, less in the past. When the working-
man had no leisure, why educate him to use something
that he would never have? The question barely arose. But

[1] The following figures of books issued in a year per head (approximately)
of the population by the urban libraries of certain counties are characteristic
but not encouraging: Cornwall 3, London (Metropolitan Boroughs) 5,
Glamorgan 6, Lanarkshire 5. One must, of course, allow for children
under sixteen and for those who possess adequate libraries of their own, but
also remember that many of these books were novels.

9

to-day it is arising, and in the near future it is likely to be urgent. In 1900 most men had enough to do to earn a living. Now, with shorter hours of work they have the opportunity to be more than bread-winners. But if the leisure of the future is to be entirely devoted to the films and the dogs, civilisation will not have gained much by it. Fifty years ago leisure was no concern of any but the well-to-do, who mostly wasted it. To-day its use is becoming a problem.

What, then, would you say of a nation which believed this, and which acquiesced in the greater part of its people leaving school at the age of 15 and being thrown straight into the deep waters of life? Would not the old proverb rise to your mind, *Parturiunt montes, nascetur ridiculus mus*? For consider what a child has learnt by the age of 15. He can read and write and do arithmetic. He has made a beginning in many subjects, and received a training which enables him to use an opportunity of learning more. But of history, except in a superficial sense, he knows nothing; of the forces that affect the fortunes of the country, which as a voter he will help to determine, he knows nothing; economics, historical traditions, political theories are a closed mystery to him; he will have opened the great book of literature but he has had little time to turn its pages; of science he is even more ignorant. Most of my readers probably did not leave school at 15; many went to the university. Let them ask themselves how it would have fared with their intellectual and spiritual life if their education had ceased at 15. Would they be willing that their own children should leave school at that age? Yet that is the lot of the great majority of children in this country. And we have been singularly complacent about it. We take it calmly, because we are used to it, and human beings see nothing wrong in abuses to which they are accustomed.

But our descendants will view it as we view the slave trade or debtor's prisons or child labour, which our ancestors accepted as natural and harmless institutions; and the sooner we anticipate the views of our descendants, the sooner we shall end a national disgrace. What is the remedy?

CHAPTER II

AN IGNORED EDUCATIONAL PRINCIPLE

We have, I believe, wholly overlooked a vital principle in education. Its neglect is largely responsible for the limited success of the education we have; and the great problem of national education will never be solved until we take it into account. The principle is: *That almost any subject is studied with much more interest and intelligence by those who know something of its subject-matter than by those who do not: and, conversely, that it is not profitable to study theory without some practical experience of the facts to which it relates.*

In some fields this is recognised. Medical students walk the wards while they study surgery and medicine; they see operations and therapy instead of merely reading about them in text-books; and the quickening of interest and understanding, which comes when they enter the hospital and see their problems in the flesh is well known. So with engineering; practical experience in the workshop is sandwiched with study of the theory. A famous firm, that used to take students direct from the university, found that a better method was to take boys into the works for a year after leaving school, and then release them for the regular university course, so that they went to theoretical training with some practical knowledge of the work. The same holds with other subjects, such as literature, history and philosophy, where it might be less expected. The most interesting—not necessarily the ablest—pupils I ever had came to the university not direct from school but after a period in the army or business or some other practical pursuit. Unlike the great majority of undergraduates who study history and literature, and even politics and ethics, when they know hardly anything of the subjects with which these deal—human nature and life—these other students had seen something of both and were better prepared to think about them.

This truth, though it has never been applied to education, was known long ago. One of the few writers on politics who always talked sense, and, while he looked at things as they are, never forgot what they should be, wrote:

One may enquire why a boy, though he may be a mathematician, cannot be a philosopher. Perhaps the answer is that mathematics deals with abstractions whereas the first principles of philosophy are derived from experience: the young can only repeat them without conviction of their truth, whereas the definitions of mathematics are easily understood.

And again,

The young are not fit to be students of politics, for they have no experience of life and conduct, and it is these that supply the premises and subject-matter of this branch of thought.[1]

In these words Aristotle says that the young are unfit to study philosophy or politics, and states his reason for thinking so. It is because they have no experience of the subject-matter of either. Philosophy and politics deal with conduct and life and human beings, and the young have seen very little of either life or men. That does not prevent them from talking about these subjects, but it diminishes the value of their opinions; they have no practical experience by which to test the truth of their theories, they repeat what they read or hear, or, in Aristotle's expressive phrase, 'they repeat without conviction' (οὐ πιστεύουσιν ἀλλὰ

[1] Aristotle, *Eth. Nic.* vi, 8, 6; i, 3, 5.

13

λέγουσιν). 'A boy cannot be a philosopher', because he has no experience of the concrete facts, on which philosophy is based: 'the young are not fit to be students of politics, because they have no experience of life.' That is, you cannot study fruitfully certain subjects, among them philosophy and politics, unless you know something of life. On the other hand there are subjects, such as mathematics, of which a boy or undergraduate is fully capable, even if he knows nothing outside the walls of his home, school or university. For whereas politics and ethics are concrete, mathematics is purely abstract and theoretic, and does not spring from life to illuminate or correct it.

These views of Aristotle are supported by the curious fact, that high achievement seems possible to the young in mathematics and in music which, depending on abstract relations of sounds, is closely allied to it. Mozart wrote a concerto and played in the Hall of Strasburg University at the age of five, Bach and Schumann were composers before they were twenty-one, Schubert in his eighteenth year wrote two symphonies, five operas and 137 songs. But how few have ever written anything worth reading on history or politics or ethics or even on literature before the age of twenty-five! What great tragedy was ever written by a young man? *Prima facie* Aristotle appears to be right in saying that politics and ethics are not studies for which the young are properly equipped.

Aristotle makes this observation incidentally in the course of his famous book on Ethics. The basis from which Newman's *Grammar of Assent* starts is the same point—our incapacity really to understand 'mental facts of which we have no direct experience'.

How shall I imbibe a sense of the peculiarities of the style of Cicero or Virgil, if I have not read their writings? or how shall I gain a shadow of a perception of the wit or the grace ascribed to the conversation of the French salons, being myself an untravelled John Bull?...Not all the possible descriptions of headlong love will make me comprehend the delirium, if I never have had a fit of it; nor will ever so many sermons about the inward satisfaction of strict conscientiousness create in my mind the image of a virtuous action and its attendant sentiments, if I have been brought up to lie, thieve and indulge my appetites. Thus we meet with men of the world who cannot enter into the very idea of devotion, and think, for instance, that, from the nature of the case, a life of religious seclusion must be either one of unutterable dreariness or abandoned sensuality, because they know of no exercise of the affections but what is merely human; and with others again, who, living in the home of their own selfishness, ridicule as something fanatical and pitiable the self-sacrifices of generous high-mindedness and chivalrous honour. They cannot create images of these things, any more than children on the contrary can of vice, when they ask whereabouts and who the bad men are; for they have no personal memories, and have to content themselves with notions drawn from books or from what others tell them.[1]

Newman carries the matter further than Aristotle, making an important distinction between two kinds of apprehension; the apprehension of something from a book or by hearsay at second-hand, and the apprehension of something at first-hand from direct experience of it, from life. The difference is between the man who knows war from Tolstoi's *War and Peace*, or Remarque's *All Quiet on the Western Front*, and the man who has been in a front-line trench; between the knowledge of unemployment, which can be acquired from a book like *Men Without Work*, and the knowledge of it possessed by the unemployed or by

---

[1] *Grammar of Assent*, p. 29.

those who live with them. Newman does not deny some value to the first kind of knowledge, but he says that it is far less intense and real than the second. In the second case we have a *real* apprehension of something of which we have had direct experience; in the first case we have only a *notional* apprehension (as he calls it) of something that we have read or heard of but never known at first-hand. (This is exactly what Aristotle means when he talks of repeating ideas 'without conviction'.) Further, while Aristotle remarked that politics and ethics cannot be properly understood without some experience of life, Newman argues that the same is true of subjects such as history and literature; that even these cannot be grasped merely from books, without some first-hand knowledge of their subject-matter and therefore that they are imperfectly appreciated by the young.

This is the gist of a famous passage, where he points out how little we understand in youth even of literature which we admire, and how its full meaning is only revealed as knowledge of life grows.

Let us consider, too, how differently young and old are affected by the words of some classic author, such as Homer or Horace. Passages, which to a boy are but rhetorical common-places, neither better nor worse than a hundred others which any clever writer might supply, which he gets by heart and thinks very fine, and imitates, as he thinks, successfully, in his own flowing versification, at length come home to him, when long years have passed, and he has had experience of life, and pierce him, as if he had never before known them, with their sad earnestness and vivid exactness. Then he comes to understand how it is that lines, the birth of some chance morning or evening at an Ionian festival, or among the Sabine hills, have lasted generation after generation, for thousands of years, with a power over the mind, and a charm, which the current literature of his own day, with all its obvious advantages, is utterly unable to rival.[1]

'When he has had experience of life.' Read Homer and Horace by all means, says Newman; feed mind and eye and ear with their images and language and music; but do not expect to understand what they are really talking about before you are forty.

This truth was first brought home to me more than thirty years ago one December day, as I walked down the road from Argentières to Chamonix after a snowfall, and suddenly from the abyss of unconscious memory a line of Virgil rose into my mind and I found myself repeating

> *Sed iacet aggeribus niveis informis et alto*
> *Terra gelu.*[2]

I had read the words at school and no doubt translated them glibly 'the earth lies formless under snow-drifts and deep frost'; but suddenly, with the snow scene before my eyes, I perceived for the first time what Virgil meant by the epithet *informis*, 'without form', and how perfectly it describes the work of snow, which literally does make the world formless, blurring the sharp outlines of roofs and eaves, of pines and rocks and mountain ridges, taking from them their definiteness of shape and form. Yet how many times before that day had I read the words without seeing what they really mean! It is not that the word *informis* meant nothing to me when I was an undergraduate; but it meant much less than its full meaning. Personal experience was necessary to real understanding.

It is a familiar phenomenon how something which we have read or heard, without paying much attention to it or seeing much meaning in it, some lines of poetry, a passage in a book, some remark of a lecturer or schoolmaster

---

[1] *Grammar of Assent*, p. 78. [2] *Georgics*, 3, 354.

or tutor suddenly acquires meaning and comes to life, because we ourselves have had the kind of experience to which it related; as though suddenly a spotlight fell on the dark background of our mind, and revealed in clear outline something lying latent and forgotten there. Among the minor effects of the Great War was an entirely new appreciation of certain aspects of those Greek writers whose writings were coloured by the Peloponnesian War. In all ages competent judges have recognised in Thucydides the greatest of historians and one of the acutest of human intellects. But it was after 1918 that we saw the real meaning of much in his political analysis; such, for instance, as

The sufferings which revolution brought on the Greek states were many and terrible. In peace and prosperity nations and individuals have higher standards because they are not involved in involuntary necessities. But war, depriving men of their easy circumstances, is a savage teacher, and brings men's characters down to the level of their fortunes.[1]

It is not that these words meant nothing to us before 1914, but their full meaning was only revealed when we had ourselves had a like experience.

It is easy to multiply examples. Take the passage where Tacitus describes life in Rome under Domitian.

Ancient times saw the extremes of freedom; we have been deprived by espionage of the right to exchange ideas, to speak or to listen, and have seen the extremes of servitude. We should have lost our memory itself along with our voices, if it had been as much in our power to forget as to hold our tongue. Now at last our spirits are recovering, but by the nature of human weakness remedies work more slowly than diseases, and as our bodies grow

[1] Thucydides, iii, 82.

gradually but perish in a moment, so it is easier to crush talent and its pursuits than to revive them. The charm of indolence creeps over the mind and we end by loving the inaction which at first we detested. Over a period of fifteen years (a long space in human life) many died from natural causes, the most active were put to death by a cruel emperor, a few of us, surviving not only others but even ourselves, passed from manhood to old age and from old age almost to the end of life's course, with our lips sealed.[1]

One read those words as a schoolboy years ago and detected their bitterness and power. But in this generation they have ceased to be literature and come to life, because Europe has actually experienced what Tacitus went through and knows now what he means: and Germans or Russians or Italians know better than Englishmen.

Or again take the close of Shakespeare's *King John*, where the French invade England assisted by disloyal nobles (the 'fifth column' of that time). Faulconbridge brings the latest news from the front.

> All Kent hath yielded; nothing there holds out
> But Dover Castle: London hath received,
> Like a kind host, the Dauphin and his powers:
> Your nobles will not hear you, but are gone
> To offer service to your enemy.

King John shows his dismay, and Faulconbridge continues:

> Be great in act, as you have been in thought;
>
> .   .   .   .   .   .
>
> Be stirring as the time; be fire with fire;
> Threaten the threatener and outface the brow
> Of bragging horror; so shall inferior eyes,
> That borrow their behaviours from the great,

[1] *Agricola*, c. 2f.

> Grow great by your example and put on
> The dauntless spirit of resolution.
> Show boldness and aspiring confidence.

Again we know how John felt and how Faulconbridge urged him to feel because we have lived through an analogous experience. For the same reason, how well we can now enter into the meaning of Wordsworth's Sonnet:

> Another year, another deadly blow,
> Another mighty empire overthrown,
> And we are left, or shall be left, alone,
> The last that dare to struggle with the foe.

To have seen something with our eyes, to have met it in life or in ourselves, is the way to understand the theory of it; and without such experience full understanding is impossible.

If our education is to be really fruitful, we must recognise a principle which has been almost wholly ignored in education—the cross-fertilisation of theory and experience. There is or should be a continual interaction between the two. No one has put this more clearly than a writer who is not generally regarded as an expert on education, though he wrote a series of famous letters about it. It would be disastrous to bring a boy up by the methods suggested in Chesterfield's letters to his son, but education would be more advanced if some attention had been paid to one passage in them:

Do not imagine that the knowledge, which I so much recommend to you, is confined to books, pleasing, useful and necessary as that knowledge is. But I comprehend in it the great knowledge of the world, still more necessary than that of books. In truth, they assist one another reciprocally; and no man will have either perfectly, who has not both. The knowledge of the world is only to be acquired in the world, and not in a closet. Books alone will never teach it you; but they will suggest many things to your observation, which might otherwise escape you; and your own observations upon mankind, when compared with those which you will find in books, will help you to fix the true point.[1]

How obviously true that is! Theory and practice illuminate each other. We know what Virgil meant by the word *informis* when we see the roofs and trees blurred with snow, but also we appreciate the effect of snow, because Virgil's eye saw and his pen described it and we have read

> *Jacet aggeribus niveis informis et alto*
> *Terra gelu.*

Because we lived through the Great War, we know what Thucydides meant when he said that 'war is a hard schoolmaster which brings men's characters down to the level of their fortunes'; but also we understand better that effect of war because we have read Thucydides. Hamlet means more to us when we have met him in life; but equally we understand the Hamlets of the world better if we have read Shakespeare's play. Only when Lear was turned out of his palace into the pitiless pelting of the storm did he understand the life of his poorer subjects, 'houseless heads and unfed sides',

> Exposed himself to feel what wretches feel.

If he could have read the passage in *King Lear*, he might have understood earlier. When we have taught we begin to see the meaning of books on education; but equally, when we read the books, the processes of education acquire

[1] Letter dated 4 October 1746.

a new meaning and its pitfalls and problems grow clear. Without theory practice is unintelligent, without practice theory is not understood.

If certain subjects need experience of life for full and fruitful study, how will this affect our educational practice? Our school population has hardly any experience of life; most university students have little more. Are their studies a waste of time? What, if anything, do they get out of them?

First note again that certain subjects need no experience of life for their full comprehension; among these are mathematics, languages, the sciences and some aspects of geography. No experience is required for such subjects. French or Latin, algebra or geometry, chemistry or physics, are perfectly intelligible, even if we have seen nothing of life or of men. They are like predigested foods, complete in themselves. With these subjects we are safe. Individuals may have no natural capacity for some of them—some children seem incapable of learning foreign languages, others incapable of any mathematics except the simplest— but these subjects are normally indicated for the young; and these are in fact subjects which the young do study. So far there is no reason to alter our present practice, or to doubt its wisdom.

But there are other subjects in the curriculum than mathematics, languages, science. There are literature, history, and sometimes economics and politics. In them the pupil studies life and human nature, of which he knows so little. Are they to be excluded from the schools, and our education reconstructed accordingly? They are staple foods in our own system, and were so long ago in the schools of Greece. Are they for adults only? Do the boy and the adolescent profit little or nothing from their study, and if so what profit do they get? Clearly they gain much, and I will now try to define the gain.

Studies lead to specific knowledge, but, quite apart from that, they are a training, varying with each subject, in the art of using the mind in kindred fields. A schoolboy, who may know nothing of the realities with which history or literature or politics or economics deal, can get this training from their study; their facts and theories are to him counters with which he learns to use his brain in these and related subjects; to argue a case and weigh evidence, to distinguish the relevant from the irrelevant, to seize the point at issue, to arrange his thoughts and marshal facts to support a theory, to discover when a statement is proved and when it is not, to reason logically and express himself clearly—in fact to play the great game of the intellect; just as soldiers playing a war game in a study with maps and flags—*belli simulacra cientes*—in some degree prepare themselves for the realities of war. All this is quite independent of any knowledge that the pupil acquires and in a sense is far more important.

The process can be seen in any university among undergraduate students of philosophy, as they play intellectual ping-pong with their tutors with the Absolute for ball. They attach little or no meaning to the tremendous conceptions which the Absolute represents, but their discussions of it may be logically impeccable, and though they may be learning little about the Absolute they are learning how to argue and discuss. They do not realise with what they are playing, but they learn to play the game correctly. Or they may write essays contrasting the English Revolution of 1688 with the French Revolution, and receive an admirable discipline in logic, relevance, order, proportion and the art of expression without ever feeling the living issues as Halifax and Churchill, Danton and Robespierre felt them; and their minds can be developed by these mental exercises, just as their bodies can be developed by physical training, though they may have no idea of the principles of physiology and anatomy on which it is based.

So it is possible for clever schoolboys or undergraduates to profit by studies of which they only see the surface. And they can and do take pleasure in them. They enjoy arguing about a problem of history or economics as an athlete enjoys running; and for similar reasons. They are using powers which they possess and they delight in exercising the quickness and acuteness and vigour of their minds as an athlete enjoys exercising his nimbleness and speed. It is an excellent and healthy occupation, and on it is founded the saying that education is what remains after we have forgotten all that we have learnt. If anyone studies a subject to any purpose, it improves the quality and powers of his mind for certain cognate uses, even if he remembers little or nothing of it.

What else does a pupil learn by studying history or literature at school? I do not wish to give a dogmatic answer to this question, but only to raise it. It is important that we should all ask and answer it, not dogmatically, not from our own prepossessions and hopes, but by observing the pupil and noting not what he is supposed to get from these studies, but what *in fact* he does get from them. My own tentative answer would be this. The child and the adolescent can learn facts—the date of the Reformation or of the Reform Bill, details of biography and history, the hard skeleton of knowledge. If we pass from knowledge to understanding—so far as the two can be separated— clearly some aspects of literature and history are within the grasp even of children. They can enjoy the music or the sonority of verse and good prose: Swinburne, *L'Allegro* and *Il Penseroso*, the songs in Tennyson's *Princess*, the hexameter of Homer and Virgil, the purple passages of Burke, Ruskin, Macaulay, Froude—the list could be extended indefinitely. They can enjoy, too, the pictures of literature and history—and how much of both is picture!—because for this appreciation they have the necessary experience, drawn from all that they have seen in city or country or sea since their eyes opened on the world. They can visualise, as clearly as any adult, the Duke of Guise in his satin dress sitting shivering in the fireless ante-room of Henry III eating *prunes de Brignolles*, or the murder of Darnley, or the ships moving up the Foyle to relieve Londonderry, or the Athenians taking their siesta in the afternoon heat on the beach of Aegospotami, unconscious of the Spartan fleet rowing quickly across the Hellespont to surprise them. Something, too, they can grasp of historic characters, so far as these come within the range of their own daydreams and childish ideals and inchoate ambitions.

Further—and even more important—if a child reads great literature or great history, their greatness forms his mind unconsciously. Some touch of their nobility passes on him, and 'wins him imperceptibly from earliest childhood into resemblance, love and harmony with the beauty of reason', of which at the moment he has no rational understanding.

They sink deeply into the recesses of the soul and take a powerful hold of it.... He who has been duly brought up therein will have the keenest eye for defects... and, feeling a most just contempt for them, will welcome what is beautiful, and gladly receive it into his soul, and feed on it, and grow to be noble and good; and he will rightly reject and hate all that is ugly, even in his childhood before he has come to the age of reason; and when reason comes, he will welcome her ardently, because this has been his upbringing.[1]

[1] Plato, *Republic*, 401 f.

So Plato describes that unconscious moulding of mind and character, which is perhaps the chief part of early education. In education, as in life, we are formed by our atmosphere without knowing it. We store up unconsciously spiritual tissue of whose nature and importance we are unaware. Later we may come to know and appreciate the influences that have formed us. For the mind is like a garden. Seeds are scattered on the soil and most are lost, but some lie inert till the outside influence of sun and moisture wakes them to activity. That is a parable of education. It scatters ideas and information on the surface of the mind; much perishes forgotten, but some seeds lie dormant till the quickening power of experience brings them to life. Hence the value of a practice too much neglected in modern education, the habit of learning great literature by heart and so storing up a treasure which later life may enable us to use. It is also an argument for certain criticised methods in religious education. It seems preposterous to teach children doctrines in which the intense thought and deep imagination of great religious thinkers have expressed their sense of the inner meaning of a world of which a child knows almost nothing, and many people would argue that such teaching was a mistake. One justification for it is that these seeds lying dormant in the uncomprehending mind will in later years be quickened by experience, and the meaning of what once seemed absurd or meaningless will be revealed. Newbolt puts the point admirably in his poem on Clifton Chapel:

> Here, my son,
> Your father thought the thoughts of youth,
> And heard the words that one by one
> The touch of life has turned to truth.

For there is in education a law of delayed action, by

which seed sown and long forgotten only grows in late years. Teachers like to see results from their efforts, and direct them accordingly. But the most precious fruits of a good teacher's work are those that he is never likely to see.

I am not trying to banish history and literature and kindred subjects from the education of the young. I am only urging that we should realise the difficulties and limitations—the important limitations—of their study in youth. To learn hard facts; to exercise powers of thought and expression; to store in the memory thoughts and ideas whose fuller meaning life will reveal; to live with models of excellence in life and thought—these are the fruits within the grasp of those who study literature, history and kindred subjects at school. But other fruits of those trees are beyond their reach. What do the great legal, constitutional, political and social issues of history mean to them? If their minds have retentive surfaces, you can plaster on to them the provisions of the Constitutions of Clarendon or the Bill of Rights, and they will reproduce these with more or less accuracy in an examination paper. But their knowledge of these things will, in Newman's phrase, be notional and not real. Parrots do not know the meaning of the phrases they repeat. Let anyone consult his own experience. We have all probably learnt the Six Points of the Chartists at school. They were plastered on to our minds, but never became part of the fabric, and, unless we have exceptional memories, the plaster has fallen off long ago. Was it ever worth applying? What can children or adolescents *comprehend* of such things? The day may come when they will have lived long enough in the world to perceive the meaning of politics, to have stood beside, perhaps to swim in, these obscure confused currents that sweep the world through political change.

Then they will understand. But that day has not dawned at the age of sixteen, or even later.[1]

Or take two other subjects, economics and citizenship, which press into the curriculum for obvious reasons. Economics are not among the great ends of civilisation, but they are among its indispensable means. They are foundations of our social order, and if they are unsound it will collapse. Citizenship is equally important, especially in a democracy. It might be otherwise if we lived in a totalitarian State, had leaders who indicated and enforced our duties to it, and did obediently what we are told. But we live in a society where men have a right to their opinions, where co-operation is largely voluntary and private judgement is respected and individual initiative is the chief motive power, and where the collective vote of thirty million voters determines the policy of the State; our machine will not work unless its component humans have some understanding of it, know what citizenship is and are aware that they are citizens. And how many electors are clearly aware even of this! So the educationist says to himself:

Here I have these children, at worst till the age of fourteen, at best to eighteen. Now is my only chance—and theirs. I must not let them escape without some knowledge of elementary economic laws, and a foothold in the vast ill-defined region of citizenship: otherwise disaster is inevitable for them and for the state.

[1] 'The study of political science is beyond the capacity, or rather, beyond the range of experience, of the schoolboy.... It requires some previous experience of life. Before you can really study the theory of good and evil in ethics, you must have realised, in your own life, the existence of moral problems. Similarly before you can really study the theory of right and wrong in politics, you must have undergone some sort of political experience... you must have wrestled yourself, in some way, with the problems of conduct and organisation which arise in human societies.' Prof. E. Barker in *The Citizen's Choice*, p. 150. The same chapter contains some admirable remarks on education for citizenship.

A very plausible argument, but the more dangerous; in it is concealed one of the greatest dangers to education. It and similar arguments drawn from the amount of knowledge supposed 'necessary to the modern man' are responsible for the overcrowded curriculum which leads to intellectual dyspepsia, hopeless malnutrition, and often to a permanent distaste for knowledge and incapacity to digest it; to the plastering ideas and facts on the surface of the pupil's mind from which they rapidly peel off; to mistaking information, which never becomes an organic part of his experience, for education which is absorbed by his mind and transforms it. The test of a successful education is not the amount of knowledge that a pupil takes away from school, but his appetite to know and his capacity to learn. If the school sends out children with a desire for knowledge and some idea of how to acquire and use it, it will have done its work. Too many leave school with the appetite killed and the mind loaded with undigested lumps of information. The good schoolmaster is known by the number of valuable subjects that he declines to teach.

I am not arguing for the exclusion of citizenship or economics from the school, but urging that we should not be too sanguine about the results of teaching them. They are remote from the experience of the pupil, who is not a citizen and who, especially in well-to-do homes, has no direct contact with the facts which economics tries to rationalise. A well-known Cambridge economist is reported to have said: 'What is the use of my talking about economics to young people who do not know the wages of their gardener at home?' Instruction in such subjects tends to be mere plaster, and in economics at least the school plasterers sometimes apply the wrong material; for it is not an easy subject even for adults.

An attempt is made to give a sense of reality to school

teaching of citizenship by imaginary sessions of Parliament or of the League of Nations, and doubtless this mimic politics, like other forms of acting, has some educational value. But no one can suppose that any idea of the atmosphere of Westminster and Geneva is given by reproducing a shadow of their formal proceedings. It may be a pleasant entertainment, but at its end the pupils will have as little sense of all that makes real politics, its vital problems, its personal ambitions, its tension, excitement, bitterness, enthusiasm, as children who dress up as doctors to visit a sick doll learn from their play about the realities of illness. And there is a certain danger that they may suppose themselves to know. In all these subjects it is better to make the pupil aware of them than to give detailed instruction in them. What would take many lessons to teach, they can equally well study for themselves in books. It sometimes seems to be forgotten that people can read after they have left school, and that if a school is unable to teach children to wish to read for themselves, it will be unable to teach them anything else of value. The demand for citizenship and economics will come in later life, when the pupil has become a citizen and from personal experience realises that there is such a thing as citizenship. The following sentence appears in the report called *The Extra Year*, published by a Joint Committee of the Association of Education Committees and the N.U.T.: 'In the senior schools it is the citizenship questions in which the parents shew most interest and themselves provide information and send up questions for answer.'[1] That is exactly what one would expect. But how strange that our method of providing the adult with the knowledge of citizenship which he both needs and desires is through lessons given to his fourteen-year-old children in a senior school!

[1] P. 115.

In one of the really good books on education, Professor Whitehead has spoken on the danger of

inert ideas, that is to say, ideas that are merely received into the mind without being utilised or tested or thrown into fresh combinations....Education with inert ideas is not only useless; it is, above all things, harmful....Except at rare intervals of intellectual ferment, education in the past has been radically infected with inert ideas. That is why uneducated clever women, who have seen much of the world, are in middle life so much the most cultured part of the community. They have been saved from this horrible burden of inert ideas.[1]

But the average pupil in the secondary school and university is not saved from the burden. The ideas are plastered on to his mind, 'without being utilised or tested or thrown into new combinations'. They can only be tested by comparing them with life, of which he knows nothing; they can only be thrown into new combinations, if there is something already in his mind with which to combine—and there is not; they cannot be utilised, for only the heat and stress of life gives occasion for their use. Our education is loaded with 'inert ideas'.

The less intelligent the pupil, the more 'inert ideas' there will be, and the more boredom in applying the mind to subjects which are dimly apprehended. Clever boys or girls learn quickly, remember well, and take a pleasure in exercising the brain. They may not—they cannot—really understand the Constitutions of Clarendon or the character of Hamlet; but they may get enjoyment and profit from talking, thinking, and memorising facts, about them. But to take this pleasure one must have, what only a minority of human beings possess, a reasonably good brain. Most people have no more wish to think for

[1] *The Aims of Education and Other Essays*, p. 1 f.

31

thinking's sake than to run a quarter-mile on a track, unless there is some obvious reason for doing it. Running and thinking for mere physical or intellectual exercise do not attract them. Hence the common failures of our education. The clever enjoy learning for its own sake; the mediocre or stupid do not. The latter, if they felt the need of science or mathematics or languages or some other subject for the practical work of life, would have a motive for study. But their school work is apt to present itself as a tale of bricks demanded by a task-master, or a dreary necessity for an examination. The teacher, an *instans tyrannus*, harries or persuades them and, if he is insistent enough, succeeds in extorting the necessary minimum. The pupils are taught—to some degree—but not educated. Anyone who has been a master in a secondary school knows these pupils; they are even to be found in universities, conscientiously walking in the treadmill or quietly evading it. They do not ardently desire education; some of them do not desire it at all. Youth does not see its uses; life will reveal them and bring the desire; but for this awakening we make no provision.

CHAPTER III

THE WAY OUT

I argued in the preceding chapter that experience of life is necessary for the full and fruitful study of subjects like literature, history, politics and economics; that therefore the cultural education of the young is and must be very incomplete when they leave school and even when they have taken a university degree—not from any fault of their own but because they have very little first-hand knowledge of life: and I suggested that these facts should be borne in mind in devising a national system of education. I now pass to consider our problem. The great mass of the population has no education after the age of 15. How can we educate it?

The obvious answer is—Raise the school age further. But the defects of our present system will not be remedied by this. I am not arguing against the raising of the school age. It may help our economic difficulties by reducing the supply of children in the labour market. It will keep children longer under influences of discipline and guidance with which they can ill dispense at 15. But the value of the raised school age is moral and economic rather than intellectual. The mind will gain something from it. The character will gain more than the mind. But even at 16 intellectual education, in any except a quite elementary sense, is only about to begin. Nobody who has seen the results of compulsory education to the age of 16 in the U.S.A. will be under the delusion that it produces an educated nation. If they compare these results with those obtained in France, where education is compulsory only till the age of 13, and where pupils can leave a year earlier if they obtain the *Certificat des études élémentaires*, they will be still further disillusioned about the intellectual advantages gained by raising the school age.

'Then raise it further and continue secondary education for all.' Those who make this suggestion cannot have considered the practical difficulties of such a plan. But if it were financially practicable, it would still be educationally ineffective. Presumably those who speak of prolonged secondary education for all are not thinking of grammar schools for the less able child, but contemplate the development, by the side of ordinary grammar schools, of something like the Technical High Schools proposed in the Spens Report, designed for boys with a practical and scientific bent and giving 'large opportunities for practical work'. But even such schools cannot, and were never intended, to omit the studies called humanistic, of which literature, history and politics are chief—the visions of human life which religion and poetry and thought have conceived, the 'study of what man is and what he should pursue', and the record of his achievements in the world. These studies are indispensable to all men as men and to all citizens as citizens, and a life or an education which ignores them is hopelessly maimed. And yet—if the argument in the preceding chapters is sound—without experience of life they cannot be studied with full profit.

Is our experience of the schools where pupils stay to the age of 17 or 18 so encouraging? With many of their pupils, and within the measure of their possibilities, they achieve their aim. But some of their classrooms present a scene of human nature either evading an unwelcome task, or struggling conscientiously but without enthusiasm with a painful duty. It is education of a sort, but hardly that education of which Milton spoke, whose 'incredible diligence

34

and courage, infusing into the young breast such an in-
genuous and noble ardour, would not fail to make many
of them renowned and matchless men'. That, or something
as near it as human nature can compass, is what we need:
but it is not what we achieve. How many of the pupils in
our secondary system would attend school, if they were not
compelled? How many learn even to care enough for their
studies to continue them in later life? How many carry
away such standards as will help them through life to
choose the good and reject the bad in literature, the theatre,
the films, life?

If this is true at present, what will it be later, if we
try to prolong secondary education for the children who
now leave school at 15? We are apt to speak and think
as if our problem were an extension of our present educational system to the masses whom it does not yet reach.
More teachers; more schools; and bring the rest of the
population into them. But it is not as simple as that.
The problem before us in 1900 was to organise and expand
an unorganised and inadequate secondary education. The
problem to-day is to educate the masses of the nation.
Those who at present receive higher education are the
better brains of the community. This is not wholly true:
there are still able boys and girls who owing to the poverty
of their parents or for other reasons have no education after
the age of 15. Still the pupils in secondary schools are on
the whole the abler children of the country, and the
majority of those who never get beyond elementary or
central school are less able. This class, which needs education and does not get it, is the problem. To bring these
children into the schools will only add to the pupils who
at present get least profit from them. We do not succeed too
well with those whom we educate now. But new difficulties
will confront us when we come to educating those with less

35   3-2

ability and weaker powers of memory, imagination and concentration. A large number of our present pupils show little aptitude or interest. It is absurd to employ methods with these weaker brethren which are only partially successful with the stronger ones.

I do not of course ignore the virtues or minimise the importance of the secondary school, which is the keystone of our higher educational system. It has its advantages and its weaknesses. Economic reasons suggest that the earlier years of life should be given to education. That is the time when the parents are most capable of earning money, and the children least capable of it. Further, it is the best age for learning such subjects as foreign languages, for memorising facts and for tolerating and even enjoying what to an adult is drudgery. Yet I doubt if any candid person, who has been a teacher or a pupil in a secondary school, feels that the returns correspond to the labour, time and money spent. How should they? You are teaching pupils in whom no intellectual faculty except that of memory and possibly imagination is fully developed, who have not, and cannot have, a full perception of the purposes and value of education, and whose eyes—and their teacher's eyes—are apt to be fixed not on its real business, but on G.E.C. or Higher Certificate, or on Matriculation or Scholarships. Some take their educational food with a healthy appetite; others attend conscientiously at mealtimes; others are compelled to swallow. But forcible feeding is not education. In every point except the economic one adult education has the advantage over secondary education. It is given to students who desire it, who have the mental development to receive it, and who have the experience of life necessary to value and interpret it; whereas secondary education is given to pupils whose faculties are not fully developed, and who have not seen enough of life fully to comprehend what education is or what it can do for them. Secondary education will always be necessary for the comparatively small class who are capable of high achievement in mathematics, science, historical or literary study. It is so firmly established in our national system that its position is not likely to be weakened. By its side will grow up the Technical High Schools of the Spens Report, or something like them. But it would be well if we became less confident that the best thing for any boy who can afford it is to stay at school till 18, and if we realised that the education of the masses can never be so achieved.

What, then, should we do? If we lived in Utopia and could reconstruct education without regard either to its past evolution or its present condition or the needs of the practical world, the ideal plan might be for everyone to leave school at 15, and pass into a system where part of the week was allotted to school, part to earning a living in some practical occupation, the proportions of each varying with the intellectual abilities of the pupil and the demands of the subjects which he was studying. Such a contact with the practical world would both sharpen the appreciation of the value and purpose of education, and, especially in the humanistic subjects, make their real meaning far more intelligible. Theory would be illuminated by practice, and practice by theory. At present the two are nearly always divorced. We lead a life of action without thought; or we think in a vacuum, without contact with the realities and problems of the world. Neither form of isolation is satisfactory.

A revolution of this kind could be made in a Platonic— or a Communist—state. It is impossible in our own. The small section of the community which proceeds through the secondary school, and thence, reduced in numbers, to a university degree, will continue to follow that beaten path. Their studies will still suffer from ignorance of life. The only possible improvement for them is that some of them may interpose a layer of practical experience between school and university by going into an office or doing some practical job for a period when they leave school. Meanwhile there remains the problem of the greater part of the nation, who in future will leave school at 15. Unless we establish a compulsory part-time continuation system which will carry them on to 18, the education of the earlier years of the youth of the nation will still be largely wasted. If we can establish such a system, they will remain in contact with those subjects to the rudiments of which their elementary education has introduced them, carrying them on to an age when the mind is growing sufficiently mature to begin to appreciate their value and grasp their meaning. Our next step, therefore, should be to put in force the provisions of the Fisher Act, and retain those who leave school before the age of 18 under some educational control —not involving whole-time school attendance—to that age. We shall thus escape their abrupt and untimely expulsion from educational influences, and we shall take them to the threshold of adult education, where the solution of our educational problem must be found.

Here we may be met by the objection that we already have adult education, but that it has failed to educate the nation. Much has been talked about it and something has been done. The *Handbook of Adult Education*, or the second volume of Mr Yeaxlee's *Spiritual Values in Adult Education*, or the volumes of *Adult Education*, give an idea of the large number of bodies concerned in it. Its great success in Britain is the Workers' Educational Association, whose history shows what a clear aim, pursued with faith and

THE FUTURE IN EDUCATION

wisdom, can create in a region without form and void. In 1950–51 there were 102,739 students in W.E.A. classes.[1] The figure is remarkable, till we remember that there are forty-three millions in this island, and that the crowd at a cup-tie final is twice as large. The W.E.A. is not to blame for that; nor indeed are the masses. It provided for their intelligentsia, and wisely concentrated on this need, instead of frustrating its own work by pursuing a variety of incon-sistent aims, and it has met the needs of a certain class of students so admirably that there is no need to enlarge on its virtues. But necessarily it has left untouched the vast mass of the population. 'A liberal estimate gives 500,000 adults at the very most as the total influenced in any direct way by any kind of organised educational activity.'[2]

Some people think that the majority are not only un-touched but untouchable, destined for ever to be the helots of the nation, exiles by nature from all but the outermost court of education, incapable of any humanistic or cultural interest. But this is not so. During the depression Queen's University, Belfast, organised classes for the unemployed and a professor who was interested in drama asked if any-one would care to act. A number of persons sent in their names; all belonged to what is known as the working class and had left school at 14; with one exception none had acted before. The first play they produced was the *Philoc-tetes* of Sophocles in translation; the second was Marlowe's *Dr Faustus*. Difficulties do not discourage Ulstermen, yet it might have seemed a hopeless task for men who had left school at 14; but the success of the performances showed how false was such a view and how completely the ordinary man can rise to the levels of the great masterpieces of

[1] These are the numbers of student-attendance; the number of individual students would be rather less.
[2] *The Handbook and Directory of Adult Education* (1929), p. 29.

literature. And every cottage gives the lie to pessimistic conclusions about his capacities, and proves that the taste for art and poetry is universal. The poorest home has pictures, however cheap, on the walls, and gives thereby proof beyond question that art of some kind appeals to all and that no one feels his life complete without it. Almost everyone enjoys some kind of music, even if it is only crooning, some kind of poetry, even if it is only a hymn, some kind of pictures, even if they are only cheap prints. Just as a baby's cries show the power of speech, waiting to be developed, so in all humans there is the latent taste for art, literature and music, capable of being trained to understand and enjoy the best. But how can it be done?

The vegetation of a district reveals the capacities of its soil, and we can find our answer by noting some new plants that have recently grown in English earth. Men's and Women's Institutes, Townswomen's Guilds, Community Centres, Unemployed Centres or Clubs, the Rural Music School, the British Drama League were created to satisfy a variety of needs, but all have, or have developed, a cultural side; they include purely humanistic studies, and they have brought them to classes hitherto unreached. These institutions or something like them may provide the education of the masses for which we are looking. Characteristic of them are the Women's Clubs. In 1926 sewing groups were started in the Rhondda Valley among the wives of unemployed miners.[1] Later, in England, and notably in Lancashire and Yorkshire, similar women's clubs sprang up in the cotton and woollen districts. They began with 'sewing, renovations, thriftcrafts and very simple forms of recrea-

---

[1] See an article on 'Women's Clubs—Adult Education from a new angle', by Helen Roberts (*Adult Education*, x, 4), from which these facts are taken. Closely analogous was the C.C.C.C. (Civilian Conservation Corps Camp) for unemployed in the U.S.A.

tion'—the object being partly to teach self-help, partly to provide some occupation and recreation in distressed areas. Then cookery, home nursing, first aid, personal hygiene and child welfare were added, and led up to 'talks on public health services, the functions of maternity clinics, and other aspects of local government'. Other subjects crept in. A programme of women's clubs in West Cumberland during the winter of 1937–8 included 'dressmaking, handicrafts, weaving, cookery, keep-fit, joinery, drama, choral singing, geography, biology, literature, psychology, European history and foreign affairs'. These developments both show the demand for adult education and suggest how it may be met. Their weakness is that, for the most part, the education which they give is casual and episodic, stray lectures or courses of lectures, stimulus rather than education, a cocktail rather than solid food. We need something more systematic and methodical.

Theories are more common than achievements in the history of education. Important and interesting as theories are, for practical purposes achievements are more instructive, since they show what is possible with human nature and in the actual world, and the educationist needs to study them even more than he studies Plato or Comenius or Herbart or Pestalozzi. Now, in the last hundred years there have been four notable achievements in education, great creations which have embodied an idea, and excited interest and exercised influence far outside the country of their origin. These are the pre-war German University, the English Public School, the Danish People's High School, and the Scout and Guide Movements. Of these the third, the Danish People's High School, should be of peculiar interest to us, for it is the only great successful experiment in educating the masses of a nation. It has reached the very classes for which we have done little or nothing. It has taught them to care for subjects like history and literature which seem remote from the man in the street. It has transformed the country economically, given it a spiritual unity, and produced perhaps the only educated democracy in the world. Here is that rare thing in education—an ideal embodied in fact. It is curious that it has excited comparatively little attention among ourselves who are facing the problem which these Danish schools have solved.[1]

We find it difficult to think of Denmark as a poverty-stricken country lacking in energy or enterprise; but such it was in the early nineteenth century, and its transformation into one of the most progressive and prosperous democracies of Europe was largely the work of the education given in these schools. The creators of the movement were a clergyman, Grundtvig, and a working cobbler called Kold—strange but most successful fellow-workers. The idea and inspiration came from Grundtvig: Kold, a man of the people, founded schools, taught, and drew men after him by strength of character and spiritual force. The first Danish People's High School was founded by a professor of literature in 1844 to combat German propaganda in Schleswig-Holstein. Others followed. In 1864 came the disastrous war with Germany. The Danish reply to defeat was to create more High Schools. In 1872 there were fifty-four; to-day there are fifty-five. They are nearly all residential, with a summer term of three months, chiefly for women, and a winter term of five months, chiefly for men. They are private ventures, owned either by the principal or by a number of persons who form a company.

---

[1] There are good accounts of these schools in *The Folk High Schools of Denmark and the Development of a Farming Community*, by Begtrup, Lund and Manniche; *Education for Life*, by N. Davies; *Denmark, A Social Laboratory*, by Mannich. See also an article in *The Yearbook of Education*, 1937.

The Government gives grants in aid. The pupils are mostly farmers and small-holders and, in a less degree, labourers. All students are over 18; the High School will not take them younger. Only 25 per cent have had anything more than elementary education; the rest have spent the years between 14 and 18 in farming or other work. There is no compulsion to attend, and no reward in the form of a degree or a diploma. The cost of living and education is about £4 per month for women, and a little more for men, and is paid by the student, but the Government offers scholarships which pay half the fees of those who could not afford to attend without such help. Yet though all the cost in most cases, and half the cost in the rest, falls on the students, it is reckoned that about 30 per cent of the agricultural community attend a High School. This is the more surprising, because they are paying hard cash for something which superficially might seem valueless for a labouring population. Though nearly all the students are and will continue to be workers on the land, there is nothing vocational in the High School curriculum. Its main subjects are literature and history. To these are added composition in Danish, mathematics, elementary science, gymnastics and (for the women) sewing. At the Askov High School the course is longer and more advanced.

My mind's eye still sees one of these High Schools within two days' journey from England. A lane through orchards leads to a large farm-like building in the country—a residential college for the ordinary man and woman. Nothing about it—except its existence—would seem strange in our own country. A few points strike the attention: the pictures on the walls, often by leading artists of the country; the place of community-singing in the curriculum (the song book of this college contained poetry new and old, including a translation of Tennyson's *Ring out, wild bells, to*

43

the wild sky); the absence of compulsion, examinations or diplomas—the students study because they wish to travel the road of learning, not to collect academic luggage labels. Such is a People's High School.

Here is a force quite unlike anything in Britain. We have, it is true, residential colleges for adult education, Coleg Harlech, Newbattle, Fircroft near Birmingham, Avoncroft near Bromsgrove (for agricultural workers), Hillcroft at Surbiton and others. But whereas we have about nine such residential colleges in a country of forty-eight and a half millions, Denmark has fifty-five for a population of four and a quarter millions. Further, the clientèle of our colleges is an intelligentsia, and their studies of a W.E.A. type. Hence, admirable as they are, they could not solve the problem of educating the masses of the nation. We have the W.E.A. But while the W.E.A. in a country with twelve times the population has some 100,000 students attending evening classes on twenty-four evenings in the year, Denmark has 5900[1] students attending for periods of three to five months continuous study. In Denmark adult education penetrates the whole nation; in this country it touches individuals and small sections.

This Danish national education has three secrets of success: it is given to adults; it is residential; it is essentially a spiritual force. Let us glance at these in turn.

The P.H.S. is a school for adults. The Danes have never attempted to solve the problem of national education by raising the school age, and most Danes leave school at 14, resuming their education in the P.H.S. after the age of 18. Grundtvig refused to admit anyone into his schools before

[1] Figures for 1952. The P.H.S. movement has taken root in the other Scandinavian countries. There are 59 Schools in Sweden, 53 in Finland and 32 in Norway.

that age. This decision was not based merely on theory, but was reached by trial and error. When the P.H.S. started, Kold and Grundtvig, the parents of the movement, disagreed. Kold supported a policy allied to that of the Hadow Report. He wished to have the pupils from 14 to 15, because, as he said, they were then still so far children that they would receive their teacher's instruction with docility. Grundtvig maintained that they should be at least 18 years old, because before that age they were too immature to think about the problems of life. Both methods were tried, and the experiment converted Kold to Grundtvig's view. The younger pupils showed neither the intelligence nor the interest of the elder. 'We got people to teach both over and under 18, and then I found out at once that we could do something with those that were 18 and over, while we could do nothing with those that were under 18.'[1] Since that day, 18 has been fixed as the lowest age at which the High School can he entered, and no Dane wishes to change the rule. Grundtvig made the discovery that secondary education for all is an easy method of wasting money and time.

'The period of boyhood is not the right school-time. Whoever is to profit by learning must first have lived a while and paid heed to life in himself and in others, for so only does he get into a position to understand books that describe life.[2]

Experience proves that the same amount of information, which it takes the half-grown youth—dozing on the school forms—three to five years to learn, can be acquired by adults, who are keen on learning *and who have done practical work*, in the space of three to five months.[3]'

---

[1] Kold, quoted in Davies, *op. cit.* p. 169.
[2] *Ibid.* p. 79.
[3] Begtrup, *op. cit.* p. 132. The italics are mine.

This sounds optimistic. Yet it has support from the results achieved in Tutorial Classes by students whose early education has been meagre, who in the mine and the factory have had no chances of acquiring the habit of intellectual work, and who bring to their studies a body wearied by a long day of manual labour. But they also bring something which no schoolboy can ever have—a fully grown intelligence, a sense of the value and meaning of education, and that practical experience of life, without which history, literature and philosophy are lifeless phantoms. For these studies, like the ghosts of the Cimmerian land, need to taste blood before they can speak to us.

A recent English experiment points the same way. In Oxford a student over the age of 23, who has attended an extra-mural Tutorial Class for three years, may be exempted from the University Entrance Examination and be admitted to the status of Senior Student, on his credentials being approved by the proper university bodies. Thus three years' formal study (consisting of twenty-four two-hour meetings per annum) is counted equal to the years spent at a secondary school by ordinary students. To admit to a university students with such limited preparation is a far more risky experiment than to admit to a P.H.S. students who have left school at 14. Yet the system works. Some at least of such students obtain first and second class honours, though their pre-university education cannot compare with that of the normal undergraduate.

The second feature of the P.H.S. is its residential life. Our adult education is part-time, an hour or two snatched from the routine of life by men and women who have already borne the burden and heat of a day of manual or clerical work. The Dane lays the task of bread-winning aside and lives for three or five months wholly steeped in the atmosphere of education; the dye sinks deeper and takes a more lasting hold. It is like a Summer School which lasts for months instead of weeks, and where the teacher, in continuous touch with his students, comes to know their needs and capacities, can adjust himself to them, and becomes less of a voice lecturing and more of a personality and an influence. Because it is residential, and because the schools are mostly outside the towns, the P.H.S. has another advantage. Contrast the dreary surroundings in which so many W.E.A. classes meet, the bare room taken for an evening in a school or institute or co-operative hall in the crowded streets of a big city, with the pleasant buildings of a Danish High School, its gardens, pictures, music, and corporate life. The one has every external attraction, the other has none. The more honour to the successes of the W.E.A.! Yet these are not the surroundings in which to pursue knowledge and deepen imagination and see visions and dream dreams of life.

Let our youth live in a healthful land, among beautiful sights and sounds, and absorb good from every side; and beauty streaming from the fair works of art, shall flow into eye and ear, like an air bringing health from a world of health, and insensibly draw the soul into likeness and sympathy with the beauty of Reason.[1]

Education is atmosphere as well as instruction; it is not an assemblage of piecemeal acquisitions and accomplishments, but the formation, largely unconscious, of an outlook and an attitude. This truth adult education in Britain has yet to grasp.

Another contrast. Danish adult education is essentially social. That is the meaning of the music. 'Stress is not laid upon the method of the singing, the real value of which lies in its power to awaken a feeling of comradeship.'[2] 'Every High School is, in a sense, a home.'[2] Such is the

---

[1] Plato, *Republic*, 401.   [2] Begtrup, *op. cit.* p. 138.

effect of the common life. Living together, the pupils learn from each other's views and personalities, from contiguity and personal talk.

I do not think that we shall succeed in developing adult education unless we make it more social. Even in education man remains a social animal. Consider how often education has burned most brightly at a common hearth, where men gathered together in company to warm their hands at its flame: in antiquity, Socrates in the market-place and gymnasium, the great classical schools of the Academy, the Lyceum, the Stoa, the Museum of Alexandria; in the Middle Ages, the universities, culminating in the residential university, recognised, at least in the Anglo-Saxon world, as their ideal form. These examples may teach us something. No doubt the lamp of wisdom can burn in solitary shrines and even in dismal lecture halls. But for the many it will not burn brightly, if at all, unless fanned by that social, corporate life which exists in a residential university and which both educates and makes education attractive.

It is as important, for practical purposes, that education should be attractive as that it should be good. For, unless it is compulsory, one of the great difficulties is to induce people to take it. This sounds cynical; but there are other good things besides education that men do not spontaneously pursue. A minority will follow knowledge for its own sake; but most people need their pudding sweetened. Even more advanced forms of education have their sugar. It is not only the studies and the degree which attract people to Oxford and Cambridge, to Reading and Exeter;[1] it is their amenities and their common life. The P.H.S. is attractive because it is residential and because the resi-

[1] I mention only these among newer universities and university colleges, because, like the P.H.S., they are largely residential.

48

dences are pleasant places. It is the Oxford and Cambridge of the poor man, and the more attractive because for its students the High School course is a rare oasis in a life of hard work and comparative isolation. Hence the importance of the residential element; I doubt whether any voluntary nation-wide system of adult education is possible without it. To attend lectures after a day's work, and regularly, week after week, to leave one's fireside for a room in one of our dismal provincial towns, which is generally much less attractive and comfortable than the local cinema, requires an effort that is only overcome by a real desire for education: and most human beings have a capacity for education, rather than a desire for it.

The third feature of the P.H.S. is equally important. To us adult education is primarily intellectual, a discipline of the intellect, a voyage into new countries of knowledge. To the Danes it is primarily a moral and spiritual force, elevating the mind and strengthening the will by the vision of great ideals. The two aims can never be dissociated; education, however intellectual, must always in some degree affect the outlook and through it character and conduct, for a man's actions depend partly on what he knows of life and sees in it; nor are ideals worth much unless they are based on and reinforced by knowledge. But the intellectual or the spiritual element predominates, according as we study in order to know or in order to act. The emphasis of the P.H.S. is on the latter. Its origin impressed this tradition on it. Adult education in England began with the desire to combat intellectual poverty, to open the treasures of knowledge to classes excluded from them. But the first Danish P.H.S. was founded with the political and practical end of fortifying Denmark against German aggression by insistence on Danish culture, achievements and ideals. That issue passed, but the aim of forming the outlook and personality of the student through an ideal has persisted. The P.H.S. is not a church (though many of its teachers were theological students at the university[1]), but it fulfils for its students something of the offices of a church by steadily insisting on a spiritual philosophy of life suited to the needs and capacities of the ordinary man. Its pupils learn something more than history and literature and some elementary mathematics and biology. They learn a way and view of life. Spiritual inspiration has been the heart of the schools since their origin. Christian Kold, the labouring shoemaker's son, who did so much to create the high school movement,

taught the young people that one can be noble-minded, even though one milks the cows or clears away the dung. He scoffed at the 'progress' which revealed itself in extravagant clothes and superficial amusements. There is, indeed, an essential difference between the ordinary democracy that aims at the attainment of a culture in mere material things and the democracy of the high schools, which strives to unite plain customs and a simple, frugal life with a genuine culture of the mind and heart.[2]

This idealism has its practical uses. In the second half of the nineteenth century Denmark, with no economic advantages, passed from depression to prosperity and became a pioneer and model of agricultural methods. The regeneration of a people is worth study, and this instance is of special interest to educationists, for it is generally agreed that the People's High School was one of the chief instruments in the economic progress of Denmark. And yet the schools seemed useless for such a purpose; they were in no sense agricultural colleges; they gave

[1] Recently 89 of the 253 teachers in People's High Schools had degrees and 53 of these were degrees in theology.

[2] Begtrup, *op. cit.* p. 102.

no vocational courses and their backbone was the study of history and literature. How strange that such subjects should produce better farming! That is the natural criticism to make and our readiness to make it explains why the results of education are so often disappointing. We give knowledge to our pupils and are surprised that some do not want it and that many others make a half-hearted use of it. Our error is that we have given them the food and do not trouble about the appetite without which they will not digest it. Our education, like our civilisation, is penetrated with an unintelligent utilitarianism, which makes us feel that we ought to be studying something 'useful'—economics, administration, modern languages, technology, etc. No one would question the indispensability of such subjects, but the prior task of education is to inspire, and to give a sense of values and the power of distinguishing in life, as in lesser things, what is first-rate from what is not. That truth, often hidden from the wise and prudent, the makers of the P.H.S. divined. They did not teach their pupils how to farm well but they produced in them a passionate desire to do it. Their aim was not to impart knowledge but to awaken intelligence and idealism. 'When they come to us, they are sleeping', said the Principal of a High School to the writer: 'it is no use teaching them while they are asleep. We try to go to the centre, to arouse the spirit—the rest will follow.'

'What is most important, is not the amount of knowledge the students acquire, but the fact that the young people get mentally and emotionally roused. They may forget a deal of the instruction; but they leave the schools different people, having learnt to hear, to see, to think, and to use their powers.'[1]

[1] Begtrup, *op. cit.* p. 38.

Nor is it only intelligence which these schools quicken. They

awakened in young men and women a yearning for knowledge and a desire to work; the character of the pupils was strengthened, and they left the schools with a much enlarged outlook on life. To satisfy its yearning for knowledge a current of youth flowed from the Folk High Schools to the agriculture schools, and when it afterwards passed out into life it did so with a strong feeling of fellowship, and a desire to work for common progress. Youth thus gained some of the qualifications necessary to the success of a co-operative movement.[1]

For this purpose they found an instrument in history and literature taught as Ruskin or Carlyle might have taught them,[2] so that their pupils learnt to know the great visions of the human mind and the attempts of men to achieve them, and went back to their work with an example and an inspiration. This did not exclude technical education. Denmark has agricultural and dairy Schools, and they are widely attended. But the P.H.S. came first and supplied the driving power. First the desire for knowledge and the inspiration to seek it: then the knowledge. So the Danes avoided the great defects of our civilisation, lack of aim and driving power. The world is full of admirable machinery, from the League of Nations downwards, which is useless because there is not the idealism or the inspiration to move it. Ideals will create machinery: machinery without ideals rusts into decay.

The P.H.S. has influenced Denmark in three ways—individual, economic, political. It has enriched countless human beings, awakening their intelligence, enlarging

[1] *Ib.* p. 48. The 'agriculture schools' are institutions for technical training in agriculture. The high school avoids anything vocational.
[2] See p. 66f.

their interests, deepening their outlook on life. Of how many Englishmen can it be said that

> Knowledge to their eyes her ample page,
> Rich with the spoils of time, did ne'er unroll!

If they had been born Danes, they would have been more fortunate. But the schools have done much more than educate individuals. They have, as we have seen, turned Denmark from a depressed country into the most successful farming community in Europe. They roused intelligence and inspired idealism; and these sought for knowledge and applied it. Further, they made possible the co-operative system on which Danish agricultural prosperity so largely depends. In British farming the co-operative movement has been a failure: mistrust of one's neighbour and individual selfishness have been too much for it. The P.H.S. is an antidote to these vices. It is easy for men to trust each other when they have lived and worked together for months under one roof; the suspicion based on ignorance melts away. The individual becomes part of a larger pattern, and a spirit grows up which checks selfishness, encourages men to feel themselves members of a community, and makes co-operation not only possible but natural.

But besides educating individuals and transforming the economic life of a country, the P.H.S. has had a deep influence on politics. 'The Danish peasantry at the beginning of the nineteenth century was an underclass. In sullen resignation it spent its life in dependence on estate owners and government officials....In the course of a century this underclass has been changed into a well-to-do middle class which, politically and socially, now takes the lead among the Danish people.'[1] This transformed

[1] Begtrup, *op. cit.* p. 32. In 1901 30 per cent of the members of the Danish Parliament had passed through the P.H.S.

peasantry became during the last century the progressive party in Denmark. It seems strange to us who expect a farming population to be conservative in politics and do not expect to find them on the Left. Again we see the influence of the P.H.S., binding people together through a corporate life, developing a sense of social equality, giving them an inspiration and the sense of a great human ideal, so that social change comes, and comes not as an economic class-war of a materialist type, with the attendant evils of immediate brutality and ultimate spiritual barrenness, but as a deliberate movement towards a higher life for men. The P.H.S. not only inspired a new order, but gave it a soul. Here it has lessons for the world on which it is needless to dwell.

The P.H.S. has achieved the task of educating a nation. Can we use its methods to solve our problem? Is something of the sort possible here? There is no difficulty in learning a lesson from two of its features: we too could base national education not on adolescent, but on adult, study; we too could make it a spiritual force, awakening and inspiring. Nothing in our circumstances makes this impossible. The difficulty arises with the residential element which, as we have seen, is a most important element of the P.H.S. (though the schools at Copenhagen and Esbjerg are not residential). Are residential colleges for adult education possible on a large scale in Britain? Conditions here and in Denmark are very different. Denmark is predominantly agricultural, England is industrial, and it is easier for a farmer or peasant to leave his work during the slack season in winter than for a clerk or factory operative to throw up his job for five months and run the risk of losing it permanently. Even in Denmark the P.H.S. has made little progress in the towns, and only 10 per cent of its students come from them. And not only is the town-dweller more tied to his work than the countryman, but he has at his door cheap amusements which compete with the P.H.S., require no sacrifice and can be enjoyed without mental effort. But education requires sacrifice and effort; those who seek it must give in order to receive, and receive in proportion to what they give. Could anything equivalent to the P.H.S. be established in this land of cities on a scale sufficient seriously to influence national life?

Only experience can answer that question, but it would be a mistake to despond. There are classes in Britain which could attend a residential college without finding them-selves unemployed when they left it; domestic servants for instance (the first Danish P.H.S. student whom I met was in service in England, and had gone home to Denmark to take a course before returning to her work). Our Government and municipalities could, if they wished, arrange to release their employees for a period. Also there are in Britain, as well as in Denmark, farmers and small-holders and farm labourers. It is sometimes said that the severer winter of the north restricts agricultural work and makes it easier to leave it for five months. But farm work does not cease in the cold weather in Denmark. It is a dairying, egg- and bacon-producing country, and cows do not milk themselves, nor do hens and pigs hibernate unfed during the winter months. Difficulties exist in Denmark too, but they are overcome, because people wish to overcome them. Consider too another point. When compulsory military service was introduced in these islands before the war, men had to leave their employment to perform it; a sacrifice actually made for military needs could also be made for other purposes, if we came to believe that education was no less important than readiness for war. If we do not believe that, we are unlikely to make a sacrifice. But it will be made, if the faith and driving force is there, and we must blame failure not on our circumstances but on ourselves. Whence shall we get the driving force?

In Britain we cannot rely on the motive that brought the P.H.S. into being. It is one of the paradoxes of history that this great educational achievement sprang not from any disinterested love of education, but from the wish to resist Germanisation and to keep the Danish language and culture alive in Schleswig in the early forties of the nineteenth century. Nationalism has never produced a nobler child, and as the P.H.S. matured, it outgrew the immediate needs that created it and shed the accidents of time and place. Propaganda became education: self-assertion passed into self-development, and the High School made not merely Danes but men. Starting from national history and literature, it has reached out into the wider history of mankind. Its students come not to maintain Danish culture but to get education, and it is established so firmly in the national tradition that Danes in the classes for which it is designed have come to regard a course at a High School much as good Moslems regard a pilgrimage to Mecca—as part of the routine of a normal life.

We have yet to create such a tradition, and we cannot find an inspiration in nationalism. Our motive must be different and we might take for our motto the saying of Marcus Aurelius: 'The poet cries "Dear city of Cecrops"; canst thou not say "Dear city of God"?' If patrotism and the desire to preserve the traditions and character of a nation can call forth the energy and determination that created these schools, are there not other motives, even more potent, to inspire them? We have to build up in England a society, where each individual, within the measure of his powers, can make the most of body, character and mind. That is an ideal as inspiring as the wish to resist German penetration.

'At Rödding School', said Kold, 'they work for Danish culture against German culture, and when the former is triumphant, the task of that school will have passed; at Hindholm they work for the rights of the peasants, and when the peasants have gained the upper hand, there will be no further use for Hindholm High School. But in my school we work for Life as against Death, and that work must continue as long as the world exists.'[1]

An extension of adult education might come in different ways. Private enterprise may found and endow colleges, as Coleg Harlech and Newbattle and Woodbrooke were founded; but that can only be on a limited scale, and the trend of politics and the financial effects of the war will reduce the number of pious benefactors. Or adult education, instead of being created from above, may grow up from below, as Women's Institutes and Women's Clubs, starting with quite different objects, have developed into an agency of informal education, and may further develop residential colleges of the Danish type. Or the State and Local Education Authorities may come to realise that without adult education the national educational system is incomplete and largely ineffective, and may take its provision seriously in hand.[2] Nothing can be done methodically, thoroughly and on a large scale until they awake to their opportunity and their duty. In the past their hands have

[1] Davies, *op. cit.* p. 119.

[2] 'While it is well that the thoughts of school men should be bent upon improving the education of children, an exclusive preoccupation on this point is undesirable, for without a concomitant or integrated program of adult education, the total public educational program must continue to be largely ineffective.' *Adult Education* (Regents' Inquiry Publication, New York State, 1938), p. 126.

been full with prior needs; with the creation of a primary and post-primary educational system, with the developments indicated by the Hadow and Spens Reports. Next presumably will come compulsory part-time education for all, long overdue and urgently required. That reform will force adult education into immediate view and make it easier to achieve. Keep people in contact with education to 18, and they are more likely to wish to continue or resume it later; and they will find it less difficult to do so. The P.H.S. has suffered because nearly all its pupils had left school at 14, and were resuming academic work after being out of contact with it for four years or longer. Part-time education to 18 will keep alive the habit of book learning, and the student at an adult school will no longer find himself among tools whose use he has almost forgotten. While our future educational development thus automatically brings adult education into the foreground, economic conditions give an exceptional chance for its development on residential lines. There will be no need to build colleges. All over the country great houses will be vacant, calling for occupation, purchasable for a song. Why should not each Local Education Authority start its own House of Education? It need not follow the exact lines of the P.H.S., if that is found impracticable. It might be used for weekends, or for weeks, of study, for educational or other conferences. Out of small beginnings great developments might grow.

CHAPTER IV

CULTURAL STUDIES IN ADULT EDUCATION

Education. But what education? The question might have been easier to answer in the age of a restricted curriculum than to-day, when art, folk-dancing, choral-singing, drama, handicrafts, health subjects and much more have taken their place with the older studies. Education is like a restaurant which used to offer a few old-fashioned dishes and now has a menu covering several pages. There are great advantages in this; the enlargement in the scope of education, the sense that it covers the whole of life, is all to the good. But there is a certain risk. For the bill of fare in these restaurants of education is not divided into any categories of courses. Soup, fish, entrées, joints, sweets, dessert are flung together in indiscriminate disorder; the customer selects but there is nothing to guide his selection, nor any suggestion that in education too there are such things as food values and order in a meal. This is a mistake. The days of widespread famine and starving intellectual appetites may still be with us to explain and excuse our indiscriminate feeding; but as famine gives way to a world in which there is food enough for all, it is desirable that we should consider whether adult education should not be more methodical than it is. But what method, and based on what?

Seen in its many manifestations, education seems an infinite number of topics, classes, techniques, standards, examinations—a Many in which no One can be discerned.

59

That is one reason why there is so much waste in it. We enter this maze with high hopes but no clear purpose and the deeper we plunge into it the more we lose any sense of direction, till we end by following our particular alley, blindly conscientious, through an *inextricabilis error* in which we have long ceased to look for a clue. Perhaps this is an unfair description of education, but most people who have taught or learnt will know what I mean by describing it as a maze without a clue. Yet there *are* clues to the maze. One clue is the old conception of a liberal education.

What is a liberal education? Most people would probably reply,

Subjects like history, literature, languages, pure mathematics and science are a liberal education, but subjects like book-keeping, business administration, commercial French, accountancy, cooking and shorthand are not. They are technical or vocational, not liberal.

So far as it goes, that answer would be true. But why are some subjects classed as liberal education and others not? In itself liberal education is an odd phrase. What has the adjective 'liberal' to do with education, and why should a 'liberal' education be regarded as a good thing? To answer that question, we must go back to the country where the phrase 'liberal education' was first used. The word 'liberal', 'belonging to a free man', comes from a world where slavery existed, and has survived into times when, in the literal sense, it has no meaning because there are no slaves. To understand it, we must imagine ourselves in the Greek world where the great distinction was between free men and slaves, and a liberal education was the education fitted to a free citizen.

That distinction may seem obsolete in a world where slavery has been abolished. But though slavery has gone, the ideal of a free man's education is not antiquated. Here, as so often, the Greeks saw to the heart of the matter and put their fingers on an essential distinction. If we had understood and remembered this idea of a free man's education, our views of education would have been less confused and we should have gone straighter to our goal. Of slaves the Greeks took little account. Their condition prevented them from being men in the full sense of the word. But they held that the free man, the real man, the complete man, must be something more than a mere breadwinner, and must have something besides the knowledge necessary to earn his living. He must have also the education which will give him the chance of developing the gifts and faculties of human nature and becoming a full human being. They saw clearly that men were breadwinners but also that they were, or ought to be, something more: that a man might be a doctor or a lawyer or a shopkeeper or an artisan or a clerk, but that he was also a man, and that education should recognise this and help each individual to become, so far as his capacities allowed, what a man ought to be. That was the meaning of a liberal education, and that is its aim—the making of men; and clearly it is different from a technical education which simply enables us to earn our bread, but does not make us complete human beings.

And what is a complete human being? Again I shall take the Greek answer to this question. Human beings have bodies, minds and characters. Each of these is capable of what the Greeks called 'virtue' (ἀρετή) or what we might call 'excellence'. The virtue or excellence of the body is health and fitness and strength, the firm and sensitive hand, the clear eye; the excellence of the mind is to know and to understand and to think, to have some idea of what the world is and of what man has done and has been and can be; the excellence of the character lies in the great virtues. This trinity of body, mind and character is man: man's aim, besides earning his living, is to make the most of all three, to have as good a mind, body and character as possible; and a liberal education, a free man's education, is to help him to this; not because a sound body, mind and character help to success, or even because they help to happiness, but because they are good things in themselves, and because what is good is worth while, simply because it is good. So we get that clear and important distinction between technical education which aims at earning a living or making money or at some narrowly practical skill, and the free man's education which aims at producing as perfect and complete a human being as may be.

This is not to despise technical education which is essential; everyone has to learn to make a living and to do his job, and he cannot do it without training: technical or vocational education is as much wanted as liberal education. But they are not to be confused. They are both important, both necessary, but they are different. And yet to some extent they overlap. Take French. A man may study it in order to be able to order his meals in a French restaurant, or for business purposes; then it is technical education. He, *as a man*, is no better for being able to talk to a French waiter, or to order goods in the French language. But he may study French to extend his knowledge of the thoughts and history and civilisation of a great people; then it is liberal education. He, *as a man*, is more complete for that knowledge. Or take carpentering: its study may be a means to a living or to making furniture or boats or other objects; then it is technical education. But it may also give a clearer eye, a finer sense of touch, a more deft hand, and in so far make a better human being;

then carpentering is liberal education. Or take Greek: it may be studied in order to get access to the wisdom and beauty of Greek literature; then it is liberal education. Or its student may have no interest in these things, but simply be taking it in order to get an extra credit in the School Certificate; then it is technical education—if it is anything. In fact as Aristotle remarked, 'in education it makes all the difference *why* a man does or learns anything; if he studies it for the sake of his own development or with a view to excellence it is liberal'.[1]

This is the kind of education (without prejudice to others) which we want—that people should study 'for the sake of their own development or with a view to excellence', so that they may become human beings in the Greek meaning of the words, and not remain mere business men, mere chemists or physicists, mere clerks, mere artisans or labourers. If so, we have a clue to the maze of education, a guide to choosing dishes from the educational menu. Whatever else we select to meet our personal tastes or needs, the dinner must include the vitamins necessary to human health, so that we achieve that liberal education which makes men fully developed, within the range of their individual capacities, in body, character and mind.

I shall only attempt to deal with a certain aspect of the liberal education of the mind (not that in practice it can be cut off cleanly from the other two). Here we enter an enormous field—that vast complex of related and unrelated subjects which fills the lecture lists of all the universities, and the shelves of the libraries of the world. This is the food which the intellect produces and on which in turn it feeds. Yet this bewildering variety can be reduced under two heads—the study of the material universe, and the study of man as a sentient, thinking and spiritual being.

[1] *Politics*, viii, 2, 6.

The first of these consists in the sciences which study and attempt to explain the material universe through Astronomy, Physics, Chemistry, Botany, Geology, Geography, and those which study man regarded as a physical phenomenon through Anatomy, Biology, and the rest. Only scientists are competent to deal with the difficult problem of teaching these to the ordinary man. The elements of different sciences can be taught—thus biology and chemistry are taught in the Danish People's High Schools—but it is even more desirable to bring home to the student the meaning and importance of science in human life. That perhaps can best be done, historically by a description of the growth of science, and biographically by some account of great men of science, their personalities and their work. This brings us to the second great branch of knowledge, of which it is a part and which is usually called Humanism. Its subject is Man—man, viewed in himself and his proper nature, viewed as literature views him, as a being with feelings and prejudices, virtues and vices, ruled by intellect, or perverted by passion, inspired by ideals, torn by desires, acting on plan and calculation or carried away by unreflecting emotion, sacrificing his life now for gold and now for an idea, an adulterer, a patriot, a glutton, a dreamer, Ægisthus, Œdipus, Hamlet, Macbeth, Faust—or man, viewed as a being governed by the laws of a universe outside him, viewed as philosophy views him, subject to limitations of time and space, of his own origin, nature and destiny, related to beings and forces outside him, adapting himself to those relations and modifying his action according to his conception of them, a creature with moral capacities or the descendant of an ape, determining his character and his future according to his wishes, or merely one wheel among many millions blindly revolving in a great machine:

or, thirdly, man viewed as a political and social being, as history views him, creating states and overthrowing them, making laws and refusing to be bound by them, opposing religion to politics, and freedom to law, binding art and politics, empire and freedom, public and private life into one harmonious whole, or crowning one to the exclusion of the rest, fighting, colonising, making money and spending it, treating his neighbour as a fellow-being, or using him as a tool for the production of wealth, monarchist, parliamentarian, socialist, anarchist, Pericles or Augustus, Cromwell or Robespierre. Before the student of literature, philosophy, and history are displayed *all* the forces and ideas that have governed man, personal, religious, or political; to see why he has rejected this and espoused that, why this failed and that was successful, what are liberty and religion, family affection and personal greed, and, in a word, to study man. As he reviews them and compares them with the present, he can see, as far as a man can see, what ideas have come down to his own day, and what new elements are combining with them, can forecast in some degree the future, and by virtue of his knowledge guide the streaming forces, and shape the molten mass, serve his country and use to the best advantage his own powers.

Merely to define history and literature is to prove that they are essential parts of every man's education. Yet to the majority of the population they are closed books. Mention poetry to the average man and he will think you slightly eccentric. It means nothing to him and has no message to him. History will sound less remote to his ears, but he will know no more of it than he may happen to remember from his days at an elementary school. How is he to be interested in these two essential subjects? If he belongs to the W.E.A. type of student, there is no difficulty;

that problem is already solved. But there is a great difficulty, if he is on a different intellectual level—and it is this type of student who must be considered if we are to have an educated nation and not merely a nation of which a minority has been educated. A walk through the poor quarters of any town and a glance at the faces of its inhabitants will remind us of the folly of treating everybody as though they were intelligentsia or even intelligent, or of supposing that methods which succeed with the few will succeed with the many. One might well despair if this problem too had not also been solved. Here again we can learn from the Danish People's High School, where history and literature are not merely subjects in the curriculum, but the basis of education, and have been made familiar and fascinating subjects to the very classes with whom we are concerned. But they are taught by different methods from those which we employ.

Contrast with characteristic lectures on a W.E.A. syllabus a typical lecture of the P.H.S.[1] The choice of the subject —Alexander the Great—and its treatment are both significant of the difference between the two. The lecturer contrasts the vigour of Alexander with the exhaustion of vital force in contemporary Greece; he shows how, unlike Goth and Hun, Alexander was civiliser as well as conqueror, and, attributing the idealist in him to his tutor Aristotle, urges that the true teacher develops the mind without weakening the character; next he describes a Danish poem on the meeting of a Brahman and the king, dealing with the corruption of Alexander's character by oriental influences, and ends with the moral that the greatness of men depends on their view of good and their desire to achieve it. Here, clearly, we are in a different world from the W.E.A.—a world of the pulpit rather than the lecture

[1] *L'École Supérieure Populaire en Danemark*, by Monnet, p. 31 f.

66

room—and the intellectual will say that this is not education at all.

Yet perhaps the Danes are right. Intellectual study has
two sides. There is the advancement of knowledge and the
ascertainment of truth, mostly a matter of minute investigation, whose results fill scientific journals and learned
literature. If it is neglected, facts are not known, truth is
ignored, and the world mistakes meteors for fixed stars and
will-o'-the-wisps for a steady light. Besides, such study has
a value of its own, as an exercise of one of the great human
faculties—the intellect putting forth all its powers and
subject to the rule of truth. But there is another side to
study, equally honourable and at least as important.
Knowledge once found, it remains to use it. Education is
a handmaid of the art of living, and to conceive it otherwise is to reduce it to a mere activity of the intelligence.
We proceed from pure science to science applied in the
service of man, from pure history and literature to their
use as repositories of wisdom and guides to life. English
literature is the contents of innumerable books and the
subject of the *Cambridge History of English Literature* in
fifteen volumes. But it is also the record of visions of life,
seen by men with rare powers of sight and expression, from
whose experience we can learn; as we can also learn from
that record of human success and failure which is called
history.

This view of history as a help to life has a respectable
ancestry. The historian of Rome wrote

The study of history is particularly salutary and fruitful
because in it you can see, in a brilliant record, illustrations
of every possible type, and from it you can take, for yourself and your state, examples to imitate and others,
disgraceful in their origin and issue, to avoid.[1]

[1] Livy, *Preface*, 10.

But, long before Livy, one of the great histories of the world had been written from this angle and with this aim, and so had become the heritage and school of a whole people. Now all these things, says St Paul, speaking of events of Jewish history, happened unto them for examples; and they were written for our admonition upon whom the ends of the ages are come.[1] So, simply and almost crudely, the apostle describes the uses of history. And in this spirit the Old Testament was written. Hence it was, and is, as fascinating to the child as to the adult, to the uneducated and even the illiterate as to the scholar. Its writers knew one side of history, the art of telling a story, and the mere narrative attracts any reader —the excitement of the stories of Saul and David, of the deaths of Jezebel and Ahab, of the wanderings of the patriarchs. But the Bible is a philosophy of history, as well as a collection of stories, and in general, if not in detail, it is the best philosophy yet written for the ordinary man. It is significant that no history has ever entered so deeply into the common mind or affected human conduct so strongly as the history of the Jewish people, as conceived and written by the writers of the Bible.

Unless they are taught from this aspect, history and literature will never reach the masses in England. That does not involve biased interpretation or distortion of the truth. But, whatever other things it may be, history is fundamentally the record of human beliefs and actions, folly and wisdom, disaster and success. The researches which appeal to scholars and students do not interest and only indirectly concern the ordinary man, and to teach these subjects to him as they are taught in universities or in the higher forms of schools is like talking a foreign language to people who neither know it, nor have the wish

[1] *See* I Cor. x. 11.

68

or need to understand it. They are not concerned with scholarship and cannot be reached through it. The most brilliant teacher is not likely to interest them in Alexander's use of cavalry or even his administrative methods in Persia. But all human beings are interested in the problem of how to live, and history will have a meaning for the ordinary man if he sees in it the faces of human beings engaged in the common struggle of humanity towards better things.

The same is true of literature and of its fine flower, poetry. Here too there is a right and wrong angle of approach: there are aspects that concern everyone and others that do not. Recently at a London settlement lectures were given on Twentieth-Century Poetry by a well-qualified university graduate. They were good lectures in themselves—for Extension or W.E.A. students—but the hearers dwindled and the unsuitability of poetry for the particular audience was apparently demonstrated. Then a working-man, with none of the qualifications of the lecturer but with a gift for reading poetry, tried the experiment of reading it, without comment, to the same audience. And, so long as he read, poetry reading remained a popular entertainment in that Settlement. The story is instructive. The ordinary man is not primarily interested in literary criticism; but he may be interested in poetry—that is, in what interested the poet. The history of literature and most of the contents of annotated editions or works of criticism have little or no meaning for him. Unfortunately it is from this angle that most teachers, trained in universities, tend to approach literature; and this may explain why the hungry sheep are not fed and do not even look up. The academic approach to poetry is a stony and repellent road for the man in the street.

Yet interest in literature is clearly natural and universal. Children—quite young ones—read. If you ask them why they like reading, you will get no satisfactory answer. But the answer is that a child lives in a little world; little in space—a certain house, in a certain part of a town; a world thinly populated by parents, brothers, sisters, a few grown-ups and other children. Reading enlarges this world enormously, taking the child into a much larger world with a much larger population; kings and queens, princesses and princes, pirates and robbers and giants, other children and other grown-ups and all their ways and lives and adventures. That is why nearly all children enjoy reading; it enlarges their world. And it is always interesting to get into a larger world.

That interest does not cease in adult life,[1] otherwise the cinemas, which minister to it, would be empty. And it is through this instinct and interest that the ordinary man can be drawn on to poetry, to other forms of literature and to history. They enlarge his world and enable him to travel through all the kingdoms of the human mind. Literature is a railway ticket, costing very little, that takes men to every country in the world, a pass that admits to the greatest of waxwork exhibitions, where every waxwork is made of flesh and blood. Do you wish to meet more, and more interesting, human beings than most people meet in a lifetime? Take the plays of Shakespeare from your shelf. Do you wish to visit the hills near Sorrento? Read Browning's *Englishman in Italy*. Or to see a famous view over the Lombard Plain? Read Shelley's *Lines on the Euganean Hills*. The visit can be made from an armchair; and besides seeing Italy, you will be seeing it with the eyes of a poet. We are on a hill top, with rooks gathering at sunrise and flying away to their feeding grounds; the green

[1] In America it has been noticed that in adult education cultural subjects appeal especially to older persons, vocational studies to 'youth or young adults'. *Adult Education* (Regents' Inquiry Publication, 1938), p. 116.

plain of Lombardy is below, and in the distance the sea
with the sun rising red above its waves, and the domes and
towers of Venice; and so the poem takes us through its
succession of sights and moods and thoughts. Nothing
except actual travel can give us such an experience, and
even travel cannot give it. For we should see the scene
then with our own dull eyes. But reading the poem we
view it through the eyes of genius and see and feel what
Shelley saw and felt in October 1818.

Literature is desirable—to enlarge experience. It is
necessary—to interpret it; to do what few, if any, can do
unaided by themselves—penetrate below the surface of
phenomena to their inner and real meaning. Poetry,
supposed to be 'highbrow' and remote, deals for the most
part with the world of everyday. Its subjects are ordinary
things seen by people who are not ordinary. A caged
thrush in a town street, a great city seen at dawn, daffodils
growing by a lake, a church, sleeplessness, blindness, a man
cabling to his wife and then crossing the Atlantic;[1] none
of these are outside the normal experience of everyone. Or
take the famous speech of Macbeth:

> To-morrow, and to-morrow, and to-morrow,
> Creeps in this petty pace from day to day
> To the last syllable of recorded time;
> And all our yesterdays have lighted fools
> The way to dusty death. Out, out, brief candle!
> Life's but a walking shadow, a poor player
> That struts and frets his hour upon the stage
> And then is heard no more: it is a tale
> Told by an idiot, full of sound and fury,
> Signifying nothing.

[1] Wordsworth: *The Reverie of Poor Susan; Composed upon Westminster Bridge;*
The Daffodils; Inside of King's College Chapel, Cambridge; To Sleep. Milton:
On his Blindness. Rudyard Kipling: *The Miracles.*

The speaker is called Macbeth, King of Scotland. But he is also anyone who has desired something, and sold his soul to get it, and finds the result disappointing. The type is familiar, though most of its representatives have pursued smaller ambitions by more innocent means than Macbeth, and none of them are masters of Shakespeare's rich imagery. Otherwise they might describe their sense of disappointment and failure in Macbeth's words, and say that life seemed a dismal and interminable procession, and that men are fools walking along a dusty road which leads to death, passing shadows, bad actors who make a brief appearance on the stage, madmen ranting loudly and meaninglessly.

Most people are shortsighted; the poet has long sight, and, where others see nothing or vague uncertain shapes, he sees life with vivid colours and sharp outlines, and enables us to see it too. That is the deepest value of poetry. We may enjoy the music or richness of its language; but its essential virtue is its revealing power. Without poetry we are more than half blind. If anyone doubts this, let him take the subjects of poems given above, think what they suggest to him, then read the poems, and ask himself if he has gained nothing. It is a gain in pleasure and appreciation: we see more in daffodils or a great church or a sleeping city after we have read Wordsworth's poems on them, and in so far we enjoy our experiences more intensely and get more out of life. But it brings a further gain—a deeper insight into life. Let anyone read the sonnets of Wordsworth written during the Napoleonic war and expressing the poet's feeling about it—'It is not to be thought of that the Flood'; 'These times touch monied Worldlings with despair'; 'Another year! another deadly blow!' and then ask himself whether they do not interpret the issues and atmosphere of such struggles and suggest the attitude in which to face them, better than the best speeches of politicians. That is what poetry does for its readers with every subject that it touches. It paints scenes on the walls of their minds that would otherwise be bare. But it also illuminates ordinary things and, like the sun in nature, suddenly fills with warmth and colour a world which was obscure and dark. To go through life without seeing it as the poets see it is to see little of it. Certainly it is not to see it in its truest light. There are many interpretations of life and its phenomena. Take for instance sex and love; Casanova saw one thing in them, Dante saw something different. Or take the scene which Shelley viewed from the Euganean Hills. A geologist would see in it certain conformations of strata, a farmer soil suitable for certain crops, an industrialist possibilities of industrial development, a historian the sites of cultures or of battles, a poet—what Shelley saw. All these interpretations of the scene are valid, yet they differ in value; the gamut runs up the scale from low notes to high; and the mark of the poet is that he interprets life more generally, more disinterestedly, more for itself and in itself, more in its permanent, and less in its fleeting, aspects, than other men. Human progress depends chiefly on what men see in life, and how they interpret it; and the ages in which the world has moved forward are those rare ages when men of religious or poetic or intellectual genius have caught sight of levels higher than those in which the world is moving. Where there is no vision, the people perish. The climax of the ruin of Zion is when 'her prophets find no vision from the Lord'.[1] Poetry is vision, and, at its best, 'vision from the Lord'.

That is why it must find a place in the education of every human being. All the science and technology in the world will not take its place; for their uses are different. Poetry,

[1] Lamentations, ii, 9.

73

with religion to which it is closely allied, is the great source of the higher interpretations of the phenomena among which we live. The saying 'I can live for three days without food but not without poetry' sounds absurd but is sense.

Adult education rightly conceived might do something to meet the most serious danger to our civilisation. The only force which in the past supplied the ordinary Englishman with clear standards and a view of life has lost much of its influence. Fifty years ago nearly everyone through readings from the Bible, in prayers, and sometimes in sermons heard once a week a great philosophy of life expounded. Much of the seed fell on stony places, much among thorns, yet, whatever the defects of ministers and congregations, it was something to have listened, even with half-shut ears, to the sacred book of the purest and greatest of religions, and the hearers learnt, if not to speak, at least to understand, a common language in thought and conduct.

The loss might not be so serious if some even partly adequate substitute had taken its place. As it is, we are far worse off for spiritual guidance than the Graeco-Roman world, which had its great popular philosophies, Cynic missionaries for the crowd, Stoics and Epicureans for the educated, preaching a rule of life. But the popular ancient philosophies were thrown out of work by Christianity, and we have no sort of substitute for religion. Modern philosophy, in so far as it is more than a technique of thought, is only available to the tiny class that understands its language. What are our equivalents for the church-going of our fathers, or the philosophies of the ancient world? What are to-day the chief constant influences on the minds of the masses of the people? They are the film and the cheap press, uttering loudly and with the confusion of many inharmonious voices such doctrines as the prospect of immediate profit inspires. It is as though some malignant deity had said a second time, 'Behold the people is one and they have all one language. Go to, let us go down and confound their languages, that they may not understand one another's speech.' These substitutes for religion will not help us to recover a philosophy of life, or teach us again to speak a common language, or even to speak intelligibly at all. Such philosophies as can be discerned in the productions of Metro-Goldwyn and Beaverbrook are not adequate guides to life.

I do not believe that our need can be fully met except through religion; but an adult education based on, or largely infused with, history and literature rightly taught might help to bring some order into the spiritual chaos of to-day and to create a democracy which had 'meat and raiment', but in which the life was more than the meat and the body than the raiment.

CHAPTER V

ADULT EDUCATION FOR THE EDUCATED

So far I have been speaking of adult education for the masses. It is our most obvious need, for at present they are not educated in any real sense at all; we cannot have an educated nation or a true democracy till they are educated; and adult education is the only road that leads to this goal. But there are other people, besides the masses. There is what is known as the educated class, in whose hands, though the composition of the class may change, the direction and leadership of the country will always rest. Paradox as it may sound, they need adult education more than anybody.

Our present theory of education—or at any rate our practice—is that every human being finishes his systematic education at a specific age; most of us at 15, the great majority of the remainder at 17 or 18, the rest between 21 and 23, and that after these ages the need for systematic thought and methodical study are at an end. It is monstrous that some 70 per cent of the population are withdrawn from all formal educational influences at the age of 15, and that we—or some of us—are comforted by the possibility that in time they may remain at school till 16, as if education was more than beginning at the age of 16. But it is almost equally absurd to regard formal education as ended when a man has been through school and university. No doubt it is better that education should cease at 21 or 22 than that it should cease at 14 or 15 or 16. But who can suppose that spiritual and intellectual growth ceases and knowledge and wisdom are finally achieved when a university degree is taken, or that the need of knowledge and wisdom does not grow more urgent with the passing of the years which bring us to positions in life when our influence on others is greatest and most momentous, influence on the state, influence on colleagues and associates, influence on dependants, influence at least on our own families, and when, concurrently, with these inevitable opportunities and duties, the cares of this life, if not the deceitfulness of riches, tend to choke the Word and it becomes unfrutiful? Consider how far—for this is the question—a graduate when he leaves the university is prepared for life. Presumably he has had a thorough mental training; that is he knows how to read (as opposed to perusing) a book, how to weigh evidence, how to tackle a new subject—in short how to use his mind, at least in the field which he has studied and in fields cognate to them. That is—or should be—the first and the most important result of a good education. Second, he has presumably acquired a background of knowledge. The world is a jigsaw puzzle, the pieces of which are put into our hands, a chaos of isolated fragments, which yet could be fitted into an intelligible and even beautiful pattern, if we had the knowledge and imagination and wisdom to do it. To the uneducated man the phenomena of the world and the incidents of his own life are separate bits of experience, which come before him singly, which he makes no attempt to combine into a whole, and in whose connections he is not interested. The educated man has had a glimpse of the design, or at least of a possible design; as each bit of the puzzle comes into his hands, he is aware that it is more than itself, and studies to fit it into its place in the whole. He has some conception of science and of what it can do; some knowledge of the history of man and of his adventures in the world; some grasp of those patterns, religious, intellectual, moral, by which prophets, poets and thinkers have tried to interpret human life—as it were, to put it together. He has got important clues to his jig-saw puzzle; he has a background to his life.

So far, so good; and if we were going to die at the age of twenty-two or a little later, all would be well. But most of us are going to live longer, and as we grow older to get into our hands increasing power—power over the fortunes it may be of the nation, of a government office, of a municipality, of a federation of employers or a trades union, of a university or college or school, of a business, of a family. In these later and most important stages of life can education do nothing further for us beyond what it did in early years? Did the need and use of it stop at 22? Were we sent out from the university finished articles, requiring simply to be seasoned by experience of life? Perhaps, if the world stood still, the answer to the questions would be yes, and education, like Baptism or Confirmation, be an *opus operatum*, which once done needs no repeating. Unfortunately, the world does not stand still. πάντα ῥεῖ is the motto of the twentieth century; everything is in a flux and, as Heraclitus said, you cannot step twice into the same river. By the time, indeed before, a man is forty, the world of his twenties will have changed, new problems, ideas, forces, methods, revealed themselves, and with all of these he ought to make his reckoning.

But can the further reckoning be made without systematic education, that is without methodical study under some guidance from experts? Some people perhaps can make it, without such study, by private reading. But private reading has its limitations: we may not always know what books to read: we cannot ask books questions nor (equally important) can they question us: and do all people read even when they can? We need at least occasional periods when we can resume our education methodically and have leisure to renew our studies, deepen our knowledge, rethink our position, and, possibly, revive our ideals. The graduate who leaves the university is like a man equipped with a new motor-car, which needs to be run-in but is otherwise in excellent condition for the road. But if he uses it for years without thorough periodical overhauls, it will cease to be a useful means of transport, and probably become a danger to the public.

And are not all of us in practice acquainted in life with such obsolete vehicles, cumbering a garage or crawling along the road? Are not all familiar, in parliament, in the churches, in education, in medicine, in government and municipal offices, in business, with men of forty years and over, whom the tide of their education carried some way up the shore and who are content to remain where it deposited them years before, who have found their way into directing posts by merit, by seniority, by mere efflux of time, who should be the pumps to drive the water of progress onward, and are at any rate the pipes and conduits through which it must pass, but who are in fact so furred and fossilised that they prevent its flowing at all? They may be men of ability and good will, they may have had an excellent education. But they are living in the world as it was when they were in their twenties, they have lost the intellectual and imaginative vigour which would have enabled them to move with the movement of the times; the pace is too much for them, it frightens them; routine, which is another name for action divorced from thought, gets an increasing grip on them; and the younger generation grumbles impatiently: 'When will they retire or die, so that we can get on?'

79

This is one of the great problems of the age, the problem how to keep the middle-aged young. It is an individual problem, but it is much more than that, for it affects social and political life at every point. For the purposes of that life the middle-aged are more important than the young; they occupy inevitably most of the key posts and directing positions in national life; and they have the experience of human nature and affairs which are indispensable for practical business and which youth in the nature of things cannot have. It would be disastrous if men were physically old in their fifties, as they used to be, but it is an even greater national loss if most of them lose their intellectual and spiritual energy by that age. In the physical realm we have solved the problem; to-day a man of sixty or seventy may be physically almost a young man, and our attention needs to be given to the even more important question of preserving his intellectual vitality, if not intact, at any rate in good repair. It can only be done in one way. The body will not remain fit if its owner leads a sedentary life; nor will the mind. But what is the regimen necessary for preserving its youth?

I can put the answer in two words—Adult Education— of a new type. At present we tend to use the term as if adult education was a means by which those who leave school early could repair the gaps in their knowledge or the deficiencies in their mental training. But it is the need of all; for all men have such gaps and defects, and the gaps grow greater as the world's knowledge advances. We need to become familiar with the idea that everyone engaged in routine or practical work, especially if he occupies a directing position, needs periods of systematic study in order to refresh and re-equip and reorientate his mind. There is no occupation or profession in which the resumption of systematic education in later life would not be profitable, and there are few human beings who would not greatly profit by it.

So far I have spoken of professional studies and argued (what hardly needs arguing) that if doctors, business men, civil servants, teachers and the rest of us had an opportunity, or, better still, recurring opportunities, to think over their occupations in later life and to study new developments and knowledge which affect these, they would go back to their work with new interest, vigour and capacity for it. But, besides purely professional studies, there are other interests common and important to all men—politics and economics, religion and the conduct of life. In all of them a man is infinitely better equipped for study after the age of thirty than he was as a schoolboy or undergraduate, for he knows so much more of human nature and the world: and each year adds to his equipment. And yet, under our present system, hardly anyone gets a chance of using it. We settle down in life with the opinions on religion, conduct and politics, that we acquired at school or university. Circumstances change, knowledge grows, and the background of our mind insensibly alters. Perhaps we make some perfunctory revision, or it is forced on us. But mainly we cling to the paraphernalia with which we entered life, never clearing out lumber or reviewing and rearranging the contents of our minds. It is not surprising if we are apt to forget what is there and to attach little importance to it. Beliefs neglected are unused.

This is especially serious in politics, and in the most important subjects of all, religion and morals. They are subjects on which the young may form confident opinions, but on which they are least qualified to do it, for the data are given by life and of life they have seen so little. In fact they accept their views from others, from home or school or from teachers or books that have struck them. These may be right or wrong. But the young, whether they know it or not, live on borrowed property, however ardently they grasp it; only in later years will they come of age and be capable of holding property of their own. No doubt people, as they grow older, make some kind of reconciliation between the opinions of their youth and the experience of life: but it is, for the most part, a rough and ready compromise, patched up as they go. And religion and morals and politics need and deserve something better —more systematic thought and study. There is truth in Plato's advice to the young: 'My lad, you are still young and time as it advances will lead you to a complete reversal of many of your present convictions; you should wait for the future, then, before you undertake to judge of the supreme issues; and the greatest of these, though you now count it so trivial—is that of thinking rightly about the gods and so living well, or the reverse.... If you will be ruled by me, you will wait for the fullness of clear and confident judgement on these matters to come to you, and inquire whether truth lies in one direction or another, seeking for guidance in all quarters.... Meanwhile beware of all impiety towards gods.'[1] Profound and salutary as is this advice, it is generally useless to give it to the young. They know better. But we might give them the opportunity of knowing better still and of judging 'of the supreme issues', as Plato suggests, in later life. Mark Twain tells a story of a man who was in prison for sixteen years, and then, trying the handle of his door, found it turn and walked out to freedom. Here is a prison in which we have long been immured and from which we can escape by simply opening the door.

[1] *Laws*, 888, tr. A. E. Taylor.

But can we open it? Such a system of adult education is obviously desirable; but is it practicable with the present organisation of our life? How are people to leave their occupations for periods of three to six months? One answer to this objection is that life might be reorganised to enable them to do it—as it was reorganised when child labour was forbidden and as it must be reorganised to permit universal part-time continued education to 18. But even under present conditions there are occupations in which a systematic resumption of education is possible, and there are cases where it already exists. There are Summer Schools on many subjects. There are Adult Education Colleges like Newbattle and Coleg Harlech (though these are for a different type of student), and, for political studies, Ashridge. Closer still to my idea are the refresher courses for doctors, and vacation courses for teachers organised by the Board of Education and, even more admirable, in some cases by the teachers themselves. But if doctors and teachers need such courses, do not other professions need them also? Are medicine and teaching the only occupations in which knowledge grows, methods improve, and human beings run the risk of stagnating?

There are certain occupations in which Adult Study could be easily arranged, and in which it seems particularly valuable, because of their immense importance to the nation, because of the continual progress and enlargement in their field, and because it is desirable that persons in these occupations should keep abreast of what is done by foreign nations as well as here. I mean the Civil and Local Government Services—in which of course are included the teachers in schools controlled by the Government and the Local Authorities. In connection with them two experiments on the lines suggested have been recently tried. The Commonwealth Fund now awards Fellowships for study in the U.S.A. to civil servants, to enable them to carry out inquiry or research on problems 'akin to those which come within the scope of the Department in which they are serving'. They are tenable for a minimum period of six months, and a maximum of twelve. In 1937 three Fellows were appointed to study respectively:

1. The system of granting patents in the United States, and its effect in encouraging new industries.
2. The place of music in American education.
3. The industrial organisation of the United States coal industry.

Here is an example of adults already engaged in professional work resuming their education. The second instance is the Summer School in Colonial Administration organised by Oxford University in 1937 and 1938 with the encouragement and help of the Colonial Office and Colonial Governments, which in its character and the breadth of its scope was a model for such purposes. It dealt with detailed problems of Native Administration but placed them in a wide general and comparative setting, including not only lectures by foreign experts on native administration outside the British Empire, lectures on local government, co-operation, education, which might throw light on these issues in our dependencies, but also lectures on general economic, political and international trends. The mere meeting of more than 160 officials, drawn from many different parts of the British Empire, and comparing their respective methods and problems, must have been an education in itself. The experiment, as one of those who took part in it said to me, 'revealed a tremendous need, whose existence we had never suspected'. Both these are instances of the practice for which I have been pleading—the resumption of systematic education by adults engaged in practical work. These instances show that the whole thing is in the air. The need for such resumed education is felt—hardly consciously perhaps—and scattered provision for it is being made; for example the Staff College established for the railways.

There is urgent need for Adult Education of this kind, and the best agencies to satisfy it are the universities, for they have the teachers, the libraries, the atmosphere and tradition of study and research. In a measure they have also the facilities. Most university bodies (notably, in the field of Social Science, the London School of Economics) have teaching and courses of the kind required. But they need to conceive such Adult Education as a regular department of their work and to push it—to do in fact in this field what they have done in the field of Extra-Mural Education. And they need also to organise definite curricula by shaping and grouping those courses which they already have and where necessary providing new ones. In most universities an adult student who wishes to study a special subject can find without difficulty what he requires. But he will be puzzled where to turn, if he requires something more than specialist study, if he is looking for a course which will place his peculiar subject in a more general setting and enable him to see it not as an isolated phenomenon, but against its background of modern civilisation; still more if he wishes to get a general view of the world problem with its many aspects, moral, political, scientific, legal. No doubt by selecting lectures from different university departments and faculties, he could get what he wants. But it is not easy, and the university should help by making the selection itself, and drawing up definite programmes for Adult Study, in which many of its existing lectures would appear.

The universities can provide the water; but they cannot

get the horses—or the right number of horses—to drink it. This is the task of the employer—in the first instance of the State and the Local Authority, because they are in a better position than any other employer to encourage the further education of their officials, and because the nation will gain most by their doing so. Already some Local Authorities have given certain of their officers sufficient leave for part-time study. Recently in the Diploma Course in Public Administration at Oxford, six of the candidates were persons between the ages of 25 and 35, holding positions in municipal, county or rural government, who had passed their technical examinations but were not graduates. Five of them took the course by part-time study, obtaining sufficient leave for this from the Local Authorities employing them, but carrying on their regular duties at the same time. But an arrangement of this kind, though much better than nothing, involves strain and prevents that full absorption of the mind which is desirable in higher studies, and the State and Local Authorities should make a regular practice of seconding, on full pay, in the first instance a limited number of their promising officials for higher study, then extending the practice as experience suggests.[1]

It will be said 'you wish to take away, for six months or a year, our best men, just those whom we cannot spare': and if 'do not wish to' is substituted for 'cannot'—there are no impossibilities in these matters—this is a frank plea. But it is a bad one. It is the plea of the poor parent who does not wish his child to go to the secondary school,

---

[1] In New York State there is a Municipal Training Institute which has training schools for persons employed in municipal administration. Between 1928 and 1936 these schools had an enrolment of over 43,000 drawn from all ranks of municipal employees. All officials receive their regular salaries while in attendance. See *Adult Education* (Regents' Inquiry Publication), p. 44 f.

because by staying at home the boy can earn money forth-with; of the business man, who wants to get his able son at once into the firm and grudges the expense of time in his further education. It is a plea which (if nature did not show its absurdity in this case) could be made against giving holidays to an efficient official. 'He cannot be spared.' He *is* spared, because otherwise he would break down; and when it is realised that periods of systematic study are as necessary to the intellectual vigour of the mind, as periods of recreation to the health of the body, such periods will be recognised as a necessity, in order to avoid a different kind of breakdown, chronic and unrecognised, from which at present many officials and offices suffer. No one would hesitate to forgo the immediate use of money, if by parting with it for six months he could earn an ample return; and, if there is any truth in my arguments, the return will be ample, and the abler the official, the ampler the return, both for the man and for the body which he serves. A man lives with details and immediate problems in the narrow deep-sunk pit of his daily work, and needs at times to climb out of it and look round; to see not only the department with which he is concerned but his occupation as a whole, and that occupation's place in the wider order of things; to remember that principles should guide individual decisions and to consider what these principles are; to study related problems and methods in other institutions and countries. Every moment the crust of routine is forming over the mind, thickening, and impairing its fertility; only a continually renewed activity of thought can break it up.

I envisage the growth of a practice by which the Government and Local Authorities will regularly second their more promising officials for periods of systematic study at the university. The growth may be slow. The more intelligent authorities will take the lead, and their reward will be not only that their officials will acquire a stimulus and knowledge, difficult or impossible to get any other way, but that the best men will wish to be their officials. Nor of course should the practice be confined to Civil and Local Government services: though it may begin with them. Some big firms already give study leave to picked employees: that is a habit which may well grow.

If the practice of resuming systematic education in later life became common, if in particular it became customary for the Civil Service and Local Authorities to second suitable officials for periods of study, a step would have been taken towards remedying a serious weakness in our national life—the neglect of the Social Sciences. There is much yet to be discovered in the field of the Natural Sciences, but no one can complain that they have been overlooked. But civilisation needs other kinds of knowledge as well, and the Social Sciences, essential if political and social life is to have a chance of being rationally built on a basis of ascertained fact, are in almost pre-Copernican darkness. How is this defect to be cured? Not by increasing undergraduate students of the Social Sciences; the undergraduate is not the person to advance knowledge. That is a task for the graduate. We must look therefore to larger endowment of the Social Sciences and to an increase of postgraduate workers in them. But we shall find difficulties in the Social Sciences which do not meet us in Natural Science. They are far more difficult subjects of study than the Natural Sciences, because to a large extent they are not laboratory subjects. They deal with human problems, and while you can isolate physical or chemical phenomena, you cannot isolate human phenomena, and therefore you cannot study them *in vacuo*—in a library or an institute—whether the subject is the

Mobility of Labour or Municipal Trading or Public Assistance or Health Services or Methods of Election or Profit Sharing or the Psychology of Politics or any of the innumerable inquiries that belong to Sociology. Books, statistics, will take you some way and give you valuable and indispensable knowledge. But there remains a kind of knowledge which the academic student can never have, but which is possessed by those who have been in actual contact with the facts themselves, by the panel doctor or the city treasurer or the election agent or the managing director. Some of them at least have information which has not found its way into books; they are in a position to collect data and to make first-hand investigation. And besides concrete facts, they have a form of knowledge which may hardly be rational or even conscious, a sort of tact or intuitive perception of things as they are which springs from living with them as they are. Unless this rich, immediate, if sometimes inarticulate, knowledge can be tapped, the study of the Social Sciences will be not only incomplete, but unreal and misleading.

It can be tapped by bringing back to the university those who have it—the civil servant, the municipal official, the doctor, the business man. This will not only add considerably to the data on which the Social Sciences must depend, and secure that cross-fertilisation of theory and practice, which is one of the most frutiful sources of advance in knowledge, but will insure against a real danger. The Social Sciences are the most difficult of all sciences, because their subject-matter, human nature and conduct, is vast in extent and obscure and elusive in character. Any suitably intelligent and hardworking person may produce creditable work in Chemistry or Physiology, and even his errors will do no serious or lasting harm. It is otherwise with Sciences which aim at directing the policy of governments and the conduct of millions of human beings. For the study of such sciences a rare combination of high intelligence, acute insight and steady common sense is needed. Their progress has been retarded not only by a failure to recognise their importance but also perhaps by a perception of their risks. Psychology for instance is regarded with a mixture of respect and apprehension, and psychologists with a mixture of interest and mistrust. Its history is strewn with the wrecks of theories, which once were the latest wisdom and now are outworn errors. Its investigations need to be assisted by every precaution, in order to avoid mistakes which may be disastrous and which discredit a study indispensable to the world. What better precaution can there be than an alliance of the laboratory worker and the practical man, in which theory illuminates and explains experience, and experience tests and checks theory? Such an alliance is planned in the most interesting and important of modern university developments. In the new Nuffield College founded in Oxford for postgraduate study it is intended that scholars and practical men shall work together. Lord Nuffield expressed his wish to bring 'to Oxford experts from the practical field to co-operate in the theoretical study of social problems'. Provision is accordingly made for the appointment of not more than twenty 'University Visiting Fellows, who shall be persons competent to assist those engaged in the University in research by giving them the fruits of their practical experience in the professions or in industry or commerce'. Nuffield College may also come to play an important part in 'Adult Education for the Educated' here suggested.

This is a new function for the university—the organisation of Adult Study, not for those who have missed education in adolescence and youth, but for those who have had it. We might expect from such developments two most important results. They would be of immense assistance to those long-overdue Sociological Studies, which should be the most important scientific development of the next fifty years. They are the only remedy for that chronic intellectual ill-health from which, generally without suspecting it, all of us more or less suffer with advancing years, because we do not take enough mental exercise.

POSTSCRIPT

SECONDARY EDUCATION: A CRITICISM

Our present situation reveals the great need of the world. If the conventional stranger from Mars arrived in Europe at this moment—after a journey through the air more hazardous than usual—he would not so much be surprised by the fact that a war is in progress, for war unfortunately is nothing new, but he would be struck by something far more serious, by the appearance of a new philosophy of life. Perhaps I should say new philosophies. But Nazism, Russian Communism and in a less degree Fascism, though differing in methods, in their ultimate character have more similarities than differences. They do not know the meaning of certain words, which had been assumed to belong to the permanent vocabulary of mankind, certain ideals which, if ignored in practice under pressure, were accepted in theory. The least important of these words is Freedom. The most important are Justice, Mercy and Truth. In Germany and Russia Liberty, Justice, Mercy and Truth, if they can be said to exist at all, have lost the meaning which civilised men have hitherto given to them. In the past we have slurred this revolution over as a difference in 'ideology'. In fact it is the greatest transformation that the world has undergone, since, in Palestine or Greece, these ideas came into being or at least were recognised as principles of conduct. Suddenly and somehow the whole bottom has fallen out of our civilisation, and a change come over the world, which, if unchecked, will transform it for generations. It is the death, or deathlike swoon, of Christianity (Lenin and Hitler knew their enemy; and the Church of Italy knows its enemy), and also of the moral and religious ideas with which Greek and Christian thinkers tamed barbarism.

This country has so far escaped the contagion, and foreign observers are right who regard England as the country that, at however great a distance, comes nearer to a Christian civilisation than any other. And yet, if our Martian had visited England in pre-war days, he would have noticed profound changes in its philosophy. What would he think of the *Daily Mirror* and other papers, or of the intelligence and energy which we devote to football pools and the like? What would he suppose to be the view of life which created those characteristic products of our era, its advertisements, films and cheap press? Even if he took up a respectable paper like *The Times Literary Supplement* and noticed how largely our novels were preoccupied with the sordid aspects of sex life, what would he suppose the conscious or unconscious philosophy of the authors who wrote and the public which tolerated them? He would suppose that it had no philosophy at all; or at least that many of its inhabitants were of the type which Plato calls the 'democratic man' and which Ibsen portrayed in *Peer Gynt*. The essence of Plato's 'democratic man' is that he has no ruling principle, no clear end, no standard by which he approves or rejects except the impulse of the moment; and his disease is that he does not know what goodness is, has no real hold on it, and so drifts to and fro. It is almost worse to have no principle han to have a wrong one. For, as Ibsen remarked, if you re really good, you may go to heaven, and if you are really bad, you may go to hell. But if you are neither, the Button-Moulder will come for you and put you into the scrap heap, to be melted down with other worthless metal. Or, if there is no button-moulder, a Hitler or Mussolini will come and do his work.

To treat a disease one must diagnose its causes, and the diagnosis of our disease is not difficult. It is a sickness of the spirit; the loss or weakening of the spiritual elements which should order life, discipline and overrule discordant or unworthy elements, and bring unity, purpose and direction into it. If so, we have to ask what this spiritual element is, where it comes from, how we can recover it.

The spiritual life of Europe, its civilisation in the full and deep sense of the word, comes from two sources, and only two, Greece and Palestine. The share of the latter is obvious, but we must not underestimate the former—no one who knows the Greek achievement will. Christianity and Hellenism, these, I repeat, are the sole sources of the spiritual civilisation of Europe. On them nineteenth-century education was based, and they penetrated and moulded the ideals and conduct of its thinkers, and very largely of all its educated men. Palestine and Greece. The first appears not only in almost every nineteenth-century thinker, including those, like Carlyle or Matthew Arnold, who rejected it, not only in reformers like Wilberforce, Shaftesbury, Maurice, Kingsley, but in the solemn Victorian portraits that ornament—or disfigure—the walls of our town-halls. It was a Christianity often heavily diluted, there was more of the Old Testament in it than of the New, its implications were not fully seized; still there was enough to give the Victorian world as coherent a philosophy as any age attains. Greece affected deeply a small class, but a very impc ant one—the men whose thought was the ferment in t ɔ life of the time. There would be little left of Mill, Arnold, Pater, Jowett, or in a later day of John Morley, L. T. Hobhouse and Graham Wallas if you took the Greek element out of them, and even men like Ruskin and Gladstone would have been wholly changed. Yes, if Christianity and Hellenism were taken out of the life of the nineteenth century and of the generation still living which was educated during it, not much would be left. For it would have lost the most important element in any age or individual—its soul. It is just the soul which is missing in our age—there is nothing wrong with its body—and I suggest that its absence or its weakness is due to the absence or weakness in our education of those influences that fed and fostered it—Christianity and Hellenism. It is not wholly missing, for those influences still persist. A small élite still learns Greek and is saturated in its literature. There are many homes and schools whose members have a chance of learning what Christianity is. And these forces have been too long in the European air to be quickly lost, and persist, as paganism persisted in the Christian era, a lingering and unconscious influence even with those who were unaware of it. But if you allow the spiritual basis of a civilisation to perish, you first change, and finally destroy it. Christianity and Hellenism are the spiritual bases of our civilisation. They are far less powerful to-day than 50 years ago. Therefore, we are losing that spiritual basis, and our civilisation is changing and on the way to destruction, unless we can reverse the process. *Hinc nostrae lacrimae*.

What is education doing to help? More, perhaps, than I suppose; but less, certainly, than it might. Cromwell described the laws of England as a 'tortuous and ungodly jumble'. That seems to me an excellent description of our education—at least of our secondary education. What an amazing and chaotic thing it is! One subject after another is pressed into this bursting portmanteau which ought to be confined to the necessary clothes for a journey through life, but becomes a wardrobe of bits of costumes for any emergency: and from time to time someone discovers a new need and points out how ignorant we are of the

U.S.A. or of our Dominions, or of Latin America and urges the inclusion of Colonial or American history, or of Italian or Spanish or Russian. And so we move towards a curriculum which recalls Burke's description of the Duke of Grafton's government—'a piece of joinery, crossly indented and whimsically dovetailed, a tessellated pavement without cement, here a bit of black stone, and there a bit of white'. And to make the chaos more chaotic, we mix the clothes together indiscriminately in our curriculum, putting on a costume and pulling it off before we have time to button it up; a period of mathematics followed by a period of French; then some science, and then some Latin, and then an hour of history and then something else wholly unrelated to what went before; so making it impossible for the luckless child to settle into anything, encouraging in him a piecemeal attitude to knowledge, turning education into lessons, as if study was a series of right-about turns on a parade ground, and not a steady and continuous advance into an undiscovered country, where each step led to a further step, and each corner turned revealed a wider view of

> 'That untravell'd world whose margin fades
> For ever and for ever as we move.'

What is to be done? What practical steps can we take? Mathematics and French and history and geography and the rest cannot be expelled from the curriculum. And children must, presumably, still learn like parrots much which they cannot understand. Only the other day I found a poor little child of 14 learning about the Treaty of Utrecht and the Pragmatic Sanction: as if at that age it was possible to envisage the rusé diplomats bluffing, bargaining, bullying; still less to have any real perception or grasp of the intricate issues involved. Perhaps it is necessary for these things to be plastered on the memory, however temporary may be their adhesion to it. But it is not enough to endure —or tolerate—the ills we have. For that will leave us where we are. What shall we do?

My first suggestion is that we should coordinate our chaos of subjects. But, how coordinate it? What common element connects the miscellaneous elements in a curriculum—mathematics, geography, French, history, science; have they any link except that they, or fragments of them, are supposed to be items in the mental equipment of an educated person, and that they appear in the syllabus of the G.E. Certificate? It is a difficult problem, and yet these and all studies, either in themselves or in the way they are taught, fall naturally into two great categories— they deal either with means or with ends. It is essential, not perhaps for the pupil, but for the teacher, to have these two categories, means and ends, in his mind while teaching; if he does this, he can turn our educational chaos into something like cosmos.

This suggestion will sound unintelligible, but it is all in the opening of Aristotle's *Ethics*, where he points out that our actions aim at an end and are means to achieving it; we cook food in order to eat, we build ships in order to sail in them, we study medicine with a view to health. Further, he points out, our ends differ in importance, and all lesser ends converge or should converge on an Ultimate End or Supreme Good—the governing purpose of life: and the more effectively our means achieve their ends, and the more certainly they are overruled by the right Supreme End, the more successful our lives will be. That is true of education as well as of life. The child comes to school to be given means and ends; to discern, or begin to discern, an ultimate end at which his activities should aim, and to learn, or begin to learn, the means which will enable him to do his work in the world; to get, or begin to get, a vision of life as a symphony or work of art in which the parts are related to the whole, in which there are many lesser purposes—such as earning a living, doing a particular job, exercising a particular faculty—but all are subordinated to a governing purpose, or Supreme End—such an end perhaps as Milton conceived when he wrote that the end of learning was 'to know God aright and out of that knowledge to love him, to imitate him, to be like him as we may the nearest, by possessing our souls of true virtue'.

It would take too long to apply this distinction of means and ends to all the subjects in education. Most of them are concerned with what I have called subordinate purposes or ends. Mathematics, for instance. The pupil learns it in order to become an engineer or an accountant or to add up marks or his house books or for some similar purpose; and also perhaps because it trains the mind. But mathematics is not concerned with the ultimate end of life; no one is the wiser about that for the hours he spends with Godfrey and Price's *Arithmetic* or Durell's *Geometry*. So with most subjects in education. Languages are not concerned with the supreme ends of life, especially if they are studied for the purposes of conversation or commerce; nor are science, or geography, or economics, or sewing, or cookery. I do not question the importance of these subjects; all are elements in the nourishment of the human being, but they are destitute, or almost destitute, of this essential vitamin. There are only four subjects in education which—if properly taught—continually confront the pupil with a Supreme End—theology and philosophy which study them directly, but with which the school is not concerned: and two subjects with which the school is very much concerned—literature, where all the visions of men are recorded; and history, where, behind the confusion ot unceasing movement, the human spirit can be discerned weaving, painfully and uncertainly, a coherent design. It is to these subjects that the school must turn if it is seeking for higher ends.

I suggest then that the best way of bringing order into this chaos of the curriculum is for the teacher to have clearly in his mind this distinction of means and ends, and the need for higher ends, to feel that he is training his pupils to live a life that is a symphony and not a series of disconnected noises—even if they are beautiful noises—to see that while they acquire the means which they need for the practical purposes of life, they should also form an idea of the end at which they should aim. If that could be done, we should have cured the chief disease of our times. If you want a description of our age, here is one. The civilisation of means without ends; rich in means beyond any other epoch, and almost beyond human needs; squandering and misusing them, because it has no overruling ideal: an ample body with a meagre soul.

Some readers may think: 'we do all this already, and in much better ways than you suggest'. If so, I withdraw and apologise: and yet I feel that this or similar teaching is not universal and that many pupils leave school without a clear end or even the sense that such a thing is necessary. At any rate University teachers are familiar with a type of boy who is well-educated in the conventional sense, but who has no clear philosophy of life, nothing to fall back on in the hours of stress, discouragement or indolence that all men experience: who is easily swept off his feet by current sophistries or the fashion of the hour, and the voyage of whose life, even if he escapes these, tends to be 'bound in shallows'. It is this type so characteristic of the age, so like this age, that ought, if not to disappear, to become more uncommon.

What kind of teaching will achieve this? It is more a matter of the teacher's attitude than of the subjects taught; and the right attitude can be found in the books dealing with education in Plato's *Republic*. The subjects in his curriculum are also in ours. But in the *Republic* they are not regarded as lessons, still less as examination subjects; they are taught, according to the Greek tradition, for themselves and for their practical uses, as they must be in any sound system; but always in the educator's mind is the sense that everything in school is there in order to contribute to the making of human beings, developed in body, mind and character, equipped for the business of living, and ruled in their aims and actions by the vision of what Plato calls the Idea of the Good. Where that spirit is present, education will succeed; where it is absent, it can never have more than partial success. The mere existence in the teacher of such a view of education—and therefore of life—will communicate itself to the pupil, though the teacher may never mention it nor the child consciously realise it until long after; for a teacher's outlook educates more than anything that he says.

But there are more definite ways of imparting a sense of ends. In earlier years—and not only then—it comes indirectly through what is read. This method is described in Milton's *Letter on Education* and earlier still in Plato's account of the education of a Greek boy: 'when he has learned his letters and is beginning to understand what is written, they put into his hands the works of great poets, and he reads them sitting on his bench at school; and they contain many admonitions and stories and praise of famous men of old, which he is required to learn by heart, in order that he may imitate or emulate them or wish to become like them'.[1] The great sources of ends are literature and

[1] *Protagoras*, 326.

history; the records of human visions of life and of human acts. Literature is one great storehouse of ends. The English are fortunate in having not only the greatest poet in the world, but the painter of the greatest portrait gallery of noble human types. This point is more important in the study of Shakespeare than Mr Verity's notes. In this connection I should like to stress the importance of learning poetry by heart and of learning the right poetry. There are few greater treasures to be acquired in youth than great poetry—and prose—stored in the memory. At the time one may resent the labour of storing. But they sleep in the memory and awake in later years, illuminated by life and illuminating it. I doubt if anything learnt at school is of more value than great literature learnt by heart. Not enough is learnt and what is learnt is often not worth learning. History is the other great storehouse of ends. Carlyle said that it is the essence of innumerable biographies; at any rate this side of it is the most intelligible and attractive to the young: and you cannot talk about any great man without immediately distinguishing two sides of him—his abilities and his ends. It is most important to distinguish them and too often they are not distinguished. The dazzling abilities of Napoleon and Bismarck blind us to the evil legacy they left to the world. I should like to see every child carry away from school portraits of a few great men of another type, as standards for judging, and touchstones for testing, human character. They must not be merely historical curiosities or the great men of a day; they must be men of all time and in the main stream of human progress; and they should represent different types of human excellence. Half-a-dozen would be ample, and every man will make a different list: my own would include Christ and Socrates, who presumably would find a place in every list, possibly St Francis, and certainly President

Masaryk. He is on a different level, and yet among the statesmen of the modern world perhaps no figure is so instructive as this coachman's son who became head of a State and who was both a practical statesman and what Plato meant by a philosopher-king. He can be studied excellently in Capek's admirable biography, *President Masaryk tells his story*.

So far, I have been concerned with a mainly unconscious habituation to right ends acquired by living with people who have had them, bringing the child into the atmosphere of spiritual health, so that a tainted atmosphere becomes repugnant to him. At early ages it is not necessary to moralise about good; it is enough to exhibit it. But, especially if the pupil stays on at school till 17 or 18, he needs something more definite. It is not only in war and politics that the English favour the habit of muddling through. They do it in life, where it is even more dangerous. There is nothing more acute or more true in Plato than his insistence that what he calls ἔθος ἄνευ φιλοσοφίας, 'habit without a settled principle', is not enough. It may be enough perhaps in an age of settled beliefs; houses built on the sand are secure in fine weather. But ours is not such an age. The rains descend and the floods come, and the winds blow and beat on us; and, unless the foundations of character go down below the sands to a granite rock of principle, a definite philosophy of life clearly seen and firmly held, the house is not likely to stand. Such philosophies you find, precise yet simple, in Christianity, and in Greece where natural religion and natural morals were born, and where their fundamental difficulties were faced with the simplicity and definiteness that we should expect from the people to whom we owe the very idea of a rational view of life.

So I would suggest that, before they leave school, those

who have not learnt Greek should be introduced to Greek thought in translation. If they are capable of thinking at all about life, they are capable of understanding the ruling ideas of Hellenism. There seems to be a curious idea that Greek is not relevant to our world. Nothing could be more relevant; for Greek made modern civilisation and is, as I said earlier, one of the two sources of our spiritual life. Greek literature *is* a view of life. Here, as nowhere else in European literature, is a clear unflurried vision of a rational human existence, which balances justly the claims of body, character and intellect, of material and spiritual civilisation, of the individual and the State. That is why the world, in ages of self-dissatisfaction, has so often turned to Greece, not to read a great literature, but to find a pattern of life; as the Roman Republic did in the full tide of conquest and material success; as the mediaeval world did, though it had the ideals and organisation of the Church; as did Mill and Ruskin and the thinkers who attempted to civilise the England of the Industrial Revolution. Greek literature contains, in textbooks on politics and ethics by men of genius, the antidote to that absence of higher ends which is our greatest weakness. Plato and Aristotle differ profoundly. Plato conceived that ideal of the dictatorship of an élite which constantly recurs in human history; Aristotle has everything of Liberalism except its weaknesses. But both regard politics as part of the indivisible tapestry of human life, where morals are part of politics and politics of morals, and where the State is conceived, not as embodied power, nor as an emporium providing for the needs of its citizens, nor as a vehicle lumbering heavily towards an unknown destination, but as an organism, all of whose parts live, moving consciously towards a higher end.

If you ask what is meant by introducing people to Greek

thought, I mean getting such knowledge of Plato as can be got from the volume of selections from him in translation which has just appeared in the 'World's Classics'. And that might be supplemented by some reading of the first four books of Aristotle's *Ethics*: or at any rate of the account of the virtues in the third and fourth books. Few things are more stimulating than to take this account, consider what we should add to Aristotle's list, what he prized and we do not, where we agree or differ from him, and how far we ourselves practise or wish to practise what he taught. Unfortunately there is no cheap and adequate translation of the *Ethics*. The best translation I know of is Mr Rackham's in the Loeb Library. Finally the pupil should be introduced to Stoicism. For Marcus Aurelius there is a brilliant introduction and translation by Jackson in the 'Oxford Translations'. But Epictetus is more bracing and more stoic.

All this leads up to Christianity, for which Greek thought, no less than the Roman Empire, prepared the way. And here we come to a difficulty. For Christians there are no difficulties in teaching it except those which belong to the teaching of a great subject. But there are teachers who do not feel certain enough about their beliefs to teach it confidently. What are they to do? My answer would be that there are certain things about Christianity which almost any intelligent, candid and serious person believes and can teach, and that anyone who does not believe them may indeed teach mathematics or science or pure linguistics, but, in schools at least, had better leave history and literature alone. For the first and the most important thing in Christianity is the actual portrait, preserved in the Synoptic Gospels, of a carpenter's son who, gathering some followers round him; taught, healed, and lived his life in Palestine, and was crucified by the Roman authorities. To see Christ so is to see Him as His contemporaries saw Him in Galilee and in Judea during His earthly life; to see what convinced the men closest to Him and who knew Him best, that he was not an ordinary man but the Son of God, convincing them not as

Light half-believers of a casual creed,

but so that they never hesitated for a moment to change their lives and to die for their conviction. That conviction of a few Jewish peasants in a minor dependency of the great and highly civilised Roman Empire seemed to most of its citizens an extravagant folly, but persisted as the Empire, apparently so stable and permanent, fell into collapse, and outlived every other creed and philosophy of the Graeco-Roman world. Thus much everyone must admit. It is a mere matter of fact. These facts do not exhaust Christianity, but they are, in the witness of St John's Gospel, the most important part of it. 'These things are written that ye might believe that Jesus is the Christ, the Son of God; and that believing ye may have life through His name.' To expound these facts, though it is not to teach Christianity, is to give the premises for it. It is to give more of it that was ever given to some of us in what were regarded as Christian schools. And anyone given so much has seen the Christian life, and the grounds of the Christian faith.

To sum up. We have lost—at any rate in the post-primary school—our grip on education. It has become a mass of uncoordinated subjects, a chaos instead of a cosmos. Its dominating idea, so far as it has one, is to provide the equipment of knowledge which an intelligent man should possess. So it tends to become a collection of isolated subjects—a world of planets, as the Greeks conceived planets, stars wandering each on its irregular way, occasionally dashing into each other. For this we need to substitute a solar system whose ruling principle is the making of human beings. Many things go to their making, but essentially it is the training of three aspects of man, body, mind and character. And neither mind nor character can be made without a spiritual element. That is just the element which has grown weak, where it has not perished, in our education, and therefore in our civilisation, with disastrous results. Nothing can be done till that element is restored. Its only sources in Western civilisation—it would be different if we were Chinese or Hindus—are Palestine and Greece: and I suggest that we may adapt and adopt as our motto the advice which Apollo gave to the Trojans. Seek out your ancient mothers. *Antiquas exquirite matres.* Anyhow the problem is there; it is the greatest of our problems; and, unless we solve it, our civilisation will perish.

EDUCATION
FOR A WORLD ADRIFT

PREFACE TO THE FIRST EDITION

England has probably never been so interested in education as to-day. There are many reasons; the obvious and increasing importance of knowledge to life; a sense of the great possibilities of modern civilisation and of its disorders and dangers; the perception that our democracy is very ill-educated; a realisation that in foreign politics between 1919 and 1939 we have thrown away a great victory with a rapidity and completeness perhaps unexampled in history and that this has been partly due to political ignorance; the need of extending education if equality of opportunity is to be more than a phrase. These considerations have interested all classes in education and forced it into the foreground. So everyone is talking about the subject, our educational system is being reviewed, and a great development of it is imminent. All this is to the good; the tide is setting in strongly and may carry us far up the shore of our need and desire. But it will not do so unless we have the right education as well as the right educational system, and we sometimes forget that these are different, though related, things.

Much of the present interest in education is political or social rather than educational. I was speaking recently about education to a large working-class audience. Their keenness was inspiring, their criticism acute and searching. But their interest was wholly in one side of the problem, in the provision of proper educational facilities, in equality of opportunity, in securing a fair chance to every child, irrespective of the position or means of its parents. They wanted more education, but did not ask what it was to teach. They were deeply concerned about the residential school, but concerned that the poor should have the same access to it as the well-to-do and not with its educational merits or defects. Their interest was in no sense mercenary; they were not thinking of education as a road to better-paid jobs: they wanted fair play for all, and they were anxious to get the educational system which would achieve this.

This attitude is natural and right. In an age of social change and in a society like our own where opportunity has hitherto not been equal, the problem of equal opportunity demands to be solved and rightly fills the mind. But there is a danger that it may overfill it, engross the attention with educational machinery and make us so concerned with providing schools that we do not consider what is to be taught inside them. Machinery is indispensable to education, but when it has been provided the bigger problem of education remains and begins. What are we to teach? At what should our education aim? What sort of human beings should it produce? These questions might interest us more.

The knowledge necessary to living must be imparted. People must be taught to use their brains. We are aware of both these needs. But there is something still more essential to which less attention is paid. Knowledge is important, still more so is the power to use it; but most important of all is what a man believes, what he thinks good and bad, whether he has clear values and standards and is prepared to live by them. Paradox as it may sound, this matters more to the making of a new world, and to its preservation, even than equality of opportunity. But of this all-important side of education—doubly important in a world of shaken beliefs and uncertain values—we hear very little. Speeches, conferences, the educational press are more occupied with educational machinery than with education. Nursery schools, raising of the school age, part-time continued education, adult study—these fill the papers, and are essential, but are not enough. As Plato said, the noblest of all studies is the study of what man should be and how he should live. It is also the most important of all studies: do we give it enough attention?

Every age has a blind eye and sees nothing wrong in practices and institutions which its successors view with just horror. The eighteenth century complacently accepted the penal laws; we have only recently discovered the absurdity and injustice of leaving three-quarters of the population without any education after the age of 14. Perhaps our grandchildren, amazed at abuses and errors which we do not notice, may say of us: 'How blind that generation was to its real problem—the human being! They boasted that science had unified the world. So indeed it had, with the result that German submarines could sink ships off the coasts of America, that wireless could carry propaganda to any country in any continent, and that men were looking forward to the day when air-craft could bomb New York from Europe and Europe from New York. They never saw that the only real unity is spiritual and that however great the advantage of being able to cross the Atlantic in eight hours, co-operation depends not on rapid transport, but on common ideals. They were conscious of the defects in their commercial and industrial system, but though their standards and values were far more chaotic, they did nothing to remedy the chaos. So their peace-time civilisation was both impressive and depressing; the unlimited means at their disposal were largely misused. Their education did little to help them. It was like a half-assembled motor-car; most of the parts were there, but they were not put together. Reformers wished to base it on science and technology, or on sociology and economics, whose importance they saw; if they had had their way, they would have produced a good chassis, but overlooked the need of an engine—not to speak of a driver who knew where to go. The real problem lay deeper than science or sociology or politics; it was spiritual. They were dimly aware of it, but, in the English way, they averted their eyes from a difficult and embarrassing question; as some sufferers from cancer avoid consulting a doctor till it is too late. It is not surprising that in the end war tore their civilisation to pieces.' There would be some justice in such a comment.

We have fine material to work on—a good racial stock, a sound national character hammered out through a thousand years on the anvil of history. In the past, spiritual forces, of which Christianity is the chief, have done much to control and direct the country, but these forces, which at all times fight an uphill battle, have lost ground; and in proportion as they lose it, life loses direction and purpose, and character becomes a habit whose roots are dead, a house whose foundations are sapped. Here is our biggest need; the need of values and standards which are more than mere habits, which go down below the soil of custom into the rock of clear conviction and are founded in a philosophy of life. The English have never been fond of the idea of anything that could be called a philosophy; they have their virtues and are content with them. But ultimately virtues depend on beliefs, and though sound habits are admirable, it is dangerous to rely on them in an age of change. Our real problem lies deeper than politics, science or economics, and in the absence of a spiritual ideal we shall never solve it. If we go on as at present, we shall probably decline into an economic religion, worshipping material prosperity in a more or less refined form. Such a religion is inglorious and, because it does not satisfy the deeper needs of human nature, short-lived.

This book attempts to raise the problem, discussing its nature (Chapter I)—how far our education deals with it (Chapter II)—the use of history and literature in forming values and standards (Chapter III)—the basis of a spiritual philosophy of life (Chapter IV). Chapter V deals with the obstacles presented by the examination system and over-specialisation; Chapter VI, with education for citizenship. I have had higher education primarily in mind, and have assumed that in the future every citizen will receive this through part-time and adult education if not otherwise; but clearly much of what is here said applies *mutatis mutandis* to elementary education.

The last chapter was delivered as the Seth Memorial Lecture at Edinburgh University and parts of the first as the Aneurin Williams Memorial Lecture. Some passages in the book appeared in an article in *The Round Table*. Professor Ernest Barker and Sir Alfred Zimmern read the book in typescript and helped me with valuable suggestions.

December 1942   R. W. L.

CHAPTER I

THE PROBLEM

A river is always flowing; over most of its reaches the flow
is so slow and peaceful that the direction of the current
can hardly be discerned and may even be mistaken, but
at times the stream bed falls rapidly and it hurries in
a turmoil of broken water. As with rivers, so with the
individual; change is always taking place, but only at
certain periods of life can it be clearly perceived. There
are times when a human being alters quickly and per-
ceptibly: we met him one summer and he was much the
same as when we saw him last. We meet him six months
later and he has undergone a visible change; he has grown
up, we say, or matured, or developed, or become old; he
has become a different being, or he is not the man he was.
So too with the State. It is always changing, for the most
part imperceptibly. You cannot, as Heraclitus said, step
twice into the same river: nor is England or any of us quite
what we were a year ago. But there come times when the
nature or the pace of change is such that no one can
mistake it. It is the fate of this generation to live in such an
age. England in the next ten or twenty years will become
a very different country from what is was yesterday, even
from what it is to-day.

If you ask me what this change is, I should say that it is
the decisive appearance of a new character on the stage:
a new class is taking a main role in the play. Our generation is seeing the same kind of phenomenon as occurred in
the fifteenth, the seventeenth and the nineteenth centuries
—a radical change. At the close of the fifteenth century

the monarch achieved a domination which lasted some hundred years; in the seventeenth century, after a moment when it seemed as if something like English democracy might be established, power passed into the hands of an upper class; with the Reform Bill the middle classes took control; to-day it is the turn of what we compendiously call 'the masses', and government of the people, for the people, is in sight, if not here. It is not an isolated phenomenon; such a change belongs to the spirit of the age; it can be seen in the Russian revolution, and it is bound to come in all educated countries. For fundamentally it is the result of education. Marx would have traced it to economic causes, and doubtless these have contributed. But the real cause is education. As soon as you begin to educate people, you teach them, however feebly, to use their reason. The more intelligent can use it effectively, the less intelligent will at any rate have an idea what the more intelligent are saying. And as soon as people begin to think, they will among other questions ask themselves: 'Why should there be such inequalities in life; in particular why should the children of some people have inadequate food, living conditions, education, etc., while the children of others, whatever their brains or character, have secure access not only to the necessities of a good life but to the superfluities of a luxurious one?' As soon as this simple question is asked by a sufficient number of people, social change begins; it is the lever which has set change in motion to-day. The answer is infinitely less simple than the question; summary solutions to the problem would only aggravate it and leave the world far worse off than it is. I do not know a solution and shall not attempt to suggest one. I merely wish to emphasise that Britain is going through a period of social and political change as great and difficult as it went through at the Reformation and in the seventeenth century and in the period of the Industrial Revolution and the Reform Bill.

The adventurous, the romantic, the heroic can count themselves fortunate to live at such a time; they are not born out of due season; the time may be out of joint but they will never say

> O cursed spite
> That ever we were born to set it right.

The majority, in whose nature these qualities are less richly mixed, may regret that they were not born earlier or later, but they may feel that this is a situation to which the words apply which Socrates used of life, καλὸν τὸ ἆθλον καὶ ἡ ἔλπις μεγάλη—'noble is the prize and our hope is great'.

Our hope is great, for the country has been through such storms before and has survived them. There were times in the sixteenth and the seventeenth and the early nineteenth centuries when things looked far darker. And the prize is a noble one. We have a great task and a great opportunity. Our revolution will not bring the millennium, which is the Mrs Harris of politicians—constantly appealed to but never seen. It may alter England for the worse; for such changes must shake and may destroy existing traditions and values, but fail to replace them by better ones. In any case, it will have drawbacks, defects and losses to set against gains. But an alteration in the balance of English life is as inevitable now as it was in the days of the Reform Bill; it has been proceeding for the las thirty years and must be completed; and it is just. Our business is to see it is carried out in the spirit of justice— not as a competition between the selfishness of the rich and the selfishness of the poor, but as an attempt to create a better civilisation. The prize is noble. This ship of

Britain carries a crew of more than forty million human beings whose future depends on the issue of the voyage, and a freight of ideals, traditions, virtues, which have enriched humanity in the past and have not lost their power or use. If we weather the storm, not only shall we preserve the ship for new voyages of wider range, but we may again teach the world the greatest of political lessons —how to carry out a revolution without bloodshed or injustice, with a minimum of hardship and a maximum of gain. In Pitt's words, we may save ourselves by our exertions and Europe by our example.

The task facing us has two sides, different though interdependent. We have to build a house for the new world to inhabit, to create the framework of material civilisation, which social and political changes require and which the new knowledge puts at our command. It is an age of science and applied science and we must make full use of them. Therefore, to profit by our opportunity, it is essential that we should have enough scientists and technologists, and equally necessary that our politicians, civil servants, business men and general public should appreciate the value and uses of science. (This is different from being actually trained in science, though it is generally confused with it; because a nation needs a sufficient supply of chemists and physicists, it does not mean that we should all be physicists and chemists.) Nor is it only scientists and awareness of science that we need. Economics, administration, foreign policy, social organisation, cannot be left to the half knowledge and bright ideas of the amateur, as they were so largely left in the last century. The foundation of the Royal Institute of International Affairs is a witness to our need; it is surprising that the need for it was not realised till 1919; and it is even more surprising that there is nothing comparable to it for the study of Social and

Political Science and that these studies should still be comparatively unorganised. When we come to provide the political, social and industrial machinery necessary, if the society of to-morrow is to express itself and function efficiently, we are likely to regret not having made systematic provision for its study: we shall be in the position of an army that takes the field without a General Staff. Expert knowledge is the obvious need of our infinitely complicated hive. So much is generally agreed; and there most people would stop. Enough science, enough economics, enough sociology, and the hive will settle down to an era of abundant and increasing honey. It might, if we were bees and not creatures of far more irrational and stormy passions, uncontrolled by mere knowledge, unsatisfied by honeycombs however full.

Our task has another side which is even more important. There is no better summary of the problem of society than nine Greek words, which in English can be translated: 'The State comes into existence for the sake of life, it exists for the sake of the good life.' This clear and simple analysis of the problem is characteristically Greek, and we should do well continually to bear it in mind and not, in our legitimate efforts to secure what Aristotle calls 'life', forget that the State 'exists for the sake of the good life'. That elementary fact is easily ignored. 'New orders' are apt to have an economic bias. But it is possible to achieve peace, material prosperity, and abolition of unemployment, and yet have a civilisation of little value: as we are reminded by Mr T. S. Eliot's epitaph on our comfortable suburbs:

A Cry from the North, from the West and from the South:
Whence thousands travel daily to the timekept City,
Where My Word is unspoken.
In the land of lobelias and tennis flannels

The rabbit shall burrow and the thorn revisit,
The nettle shall flourish on the gravel court,
And the wind shall say: 'Here were decent godless people:
Their only monument the asphalt road
And a thousand lost golf balls.'

Here the spread of democracy will not necessarily help us; indeed it makes our task more difficult. To call the masses into power is to dilute existing culture. They must be humoured and satisfied; attention must be paid to their interests and tastes, and if these are trifling, ignoble and base, the level of civilisation will fall. There is good democracy: there is also the democracy which Mussolini described as 'a social order in which a degenerate mass has no other care than to enjoy the ignoble pleasures of vulgar men'; as it was said of the masses under the Roman Empire that 'the once sovereign people has thrown its cares to the winds, limits its ambitions and only asks anxiously for two things, bread and the games of the Circus'.[1] It is easy to translate *panem et Circenses* into modern equivalents—free bread and free amusements, doles and the dogs. The spread of democracy may mean cultural decline. Plato said: 'Political constitutions are made not from wood and stone but from the dispositions of their citizens, which turn the scale and draw everything in their wake',[2] and already we have seen the influence of the masses drawing our civilisation in their wake. The newspapers of to-day with the biggest circulation are on a lower level than any published fifty years ago. In the last century there were no football pools, no nation-wide organisation of betting, no litter nuisance; the drama may have been poor, but it did not fall so low as most films of our time. Do not blame the masses for this; blame the newspaper proprietors, the film magnates, the organisers

[1] Juvenal, 10. 80.   [2] *Republic*, 544.

of pools; and let us blame ourselves, who have left the masses without the higher education which might have given them an antidote to the poison. We have called a new class on to the stage, but done little to prepare it for its role.

The clearest condemnation of our pre-war civilisation is that though the war has destroyed much of it, we have little to regret except some beautiful buildings, and are a better people leading better lives than in peace. If our civilisation disappeared utterly, and archaeologists excavating our rubbish heaps 1000 years hence had to reconstruct it from the remains of the cheap newspapers, films and advertisements, which reflect the amusements and desires of most of the population, they would probably class the pre-war world with the decadence of the Roman Empire. Comparing us with the Middle Ages which built cathedrals and churches, they would label the twentieth century 'the cinema-building age'. If the reviews of novels in that admirable paper *The Times Literary Supplement* had survived to show the tastes of the educated class, the future historian would be surprised at a society apparently interested by a succession of sex adventures, books on Byron's 'loves', and biographies of the major and minor courtesans of history: he might suppose that, though presumably all of our novelists had read Shakespeare and some had read Homer, many of them found their ideal of woman in the unchaste maidservants of Odysseus rather than in Nausicaa and Penelope, in Cressida and Helen rather than in Portia or Beatrice: and he might head his chapter on pre-war novels with the contemptuous comment of Thersites in *Troilus and Cressida*: 'What's become of the wenching rogues?...But in a sort lechery eats itself.' Certainly he would wonder that Shakespeare's nation produced so many writers who were without his sense of good and evil;

and ask why, in the crisis of European civilisation, the intellectuals ridiculed, denounced or deplored the weaknesses of their time but had not the faith or constructive power to see a vision of better things that might have renewed it.

No doubt I am putting one side of the case. But it is a very important side. If we were looking for a catchword to describe our age, various phrases would occur to the mind: we might call it the Age of Science, or the Age of Social Revolution, or the Age without Standards. None would be exhaustive, none quite just; but the last would have some claim to consideration. That may seem a hard judgement. For our age has great virtues; they were present in peace, they have been revealed to the world and to ourselves by the war. Our weakness is that good and evil are mixed together and that the tares not only grow among the wheat but are not distinguished from it. Look at any issue of our cheap daily papers in peace-time and you will see what I mean; or take an instance from *Life*, a journal which has excellent and serious articles in it, and then, among all this first-rate matter, the following description of a popular entertainment: 'His formula for production is to hire top-notch stars and composers, set them off in a gilt-edged production, keep the comedy loud and lewd. By this formula Mr —'s shows are now grossing over $90,000 a week.' That is American; but this description applies to other besides American shows. To what degradation has a society fallen, which not only has such amusements but speaks of them without a sense of shame; among whose characteristic phrase-coinages are 'strip-tease' and 'sex-appeal'! How strange that such things should appear, without any sense of incongruity, in a high-class paper! That is what I mean by saying that this generation might be called 'The Age without Standards'.

The life without standards exists in all epochs, but it is the peculiar danger of a rich society at whose feet every kind of facility, distraction and pleasure are poured in indiscriminate profusion. Commercialism helps the chaos. For the aim of commerce is not to sell what is best for people or even what they really need, but simply to sell: its final standard is successful sale. Such a society breeds the type which Plato calls the 'democratic' man, behind the lineaments of whose portrait, drawn more than 2000 years ago, we discern a contemporary face:

He spends as much time and pains and money on his superfluous pleasures as on the necessary ones....He sets all his pleasures on a footing of equality, denying to none equal rights and maintenance, and allowing each in turn, as it presents itself, to succeed to the government of his soul until it is satisfied. When he is told that some pleasures should be pursued and valued as arising from desires of a higher order, others chastised and enslaved because the desires are base, he will shut the gates of the citadel against the messengers of truth, shaking his head and declaring that one appetite is as good as another and all must have their equal rights. So he spends his days indulging the pleasure of the moment, now intoxicated with wine and music, and then taking to a spare diet and drinking nothing but water; one day in hard training, the next doing nothing at all, the third apparently immersed in study. Every now and then he takes a part in politics, and jumps to his feet to say or do whatever comes into his head. Or he will set out to rival someone whom he admires, a soldier perhaps, or, if the fancy takes him, a man of business.[1]

Such a character is not wholly bad. It has moments of energy and intermittent spurts of goodness, but the desire

[1] *Republic,* 561.

or ambition of the moment masters it—now sex, now money, now something else, and it makes no distinction between good and bad, because it has no standards, no principle to rule and discipline it. 'Such a man's life', as Plato says, 'is subject to no order or restraint, and he has no wish to change an existence which he calls pleasant, free and happy.' But of all lives the life without standards is the most ignoble and barren, sweet in the mouth but bitter in the belly.

In this portrait of a fourth-century Athenian we see a phenomenon of our own age, the same indiscriminate mixture of good and bad, everything by turns and nothing long; as if the world was a department store, where men wandered from counter to counter, buying now goods of the highest quality and now mere junk. That is our peacetime world; not a civilisation but the raw material of one, something wholly inadequate either to the resources at our command or to the capacities of human nature, a moral anarchy waiting for some overruling ideal to discipline and order it. Without such an ideal we play a game of blind man's buff, where the blind player, plucked this way and that, turns irresolutely first in one direction, then in another and catches nobody. That weakness extends from life at home to policy abroad. Here, the autocracies have had the quick decision and concentrated energy which spring from a clearly seen ideal and are impossible without it. What have been the marks of England and America in their pre-war years? Slowness to move, wavering purpose, uncertainty of aim, 'safety first'. The initiative has been with others, and we have waited till they forced us to decide and act. In the struggle between Germany and the democratic countries 'something whole-hearted has faced the half-hearted' and our weakness has imperilled and still imperils not only the things we hold dearest but the future of the world. Democracy has not commanded the spiritual forces necessary for its task or even for its safety. It is not our fortune, or democracy, or even its political leaders that are to blame. The fault lies far deeper: it

> is not in our stars
> But in ourselves, that we are underlings.

'To will anything thoroughly', says a modern writer, 'demands asceticism, that is life-long devotion to a single ideal carefully selected.... Will always conquers culture, when it is mere culture and not Christianity which brings concentration, determination, energy and supernatural reinforcement.'[1] The Germans have had the single ideal, the asceticism, the will; we have had culture without Christianity; or—for that is too hard a judgement—our will and our religion have been impaired, overlaid and confused. For the moment war has disciplined us, imposing standards and forcibly cutting out of life things which in peace-time disgraced it, compelling us to understand the saying 'Strait is the gate and narrow is the way which leads to life'. We have accepted perforce the narrowing of our way, and so far are nearer to the road to life. The country is united for a great purpose, in which no doubt our interests are involved but which far transcends them, and for which practically every member of the nation is ready to sacrifice pleasure, comfort, ease and life—many have sacrificed all. If that spirit lasted after the war, what an England, what a world we might have! But will it last when the urgency passes and the road broadens and we can walk where and as we will?

There we have the major task of this generation; how to find a principle to rule life, and firm footing in the turbid flux of modern civilisation with its films, its motor

---

[1] Foerster, *Europe and the German Question*, p. 70.

cars, its advertisements, its commercialism, its showy and seductive abundance of all that the childish, acquisitive heart of man desires.

To be successful, we must realise that we are in the midst of two revolutions: a social and economic and political revolution; but also a spiritual revolution—the weakening or dissolution of the traditions and beliefs which for many centuries have ruled Western civilisation and held it together. This revolution has been partly assisted and partly concealed from us by other shocks and revolutions which pressed more insistently on the attention; by the war; by class conflict and social change; by science transforming the economic system, disclosing possibilities which outrun imagination, and suggesting a new, materialist interpretation of life (which, however, is as old as the fourth century B.C.).

Throughout the nineteenth century, England had, so far as any country ever had such a thing, a definite philosophy of life, to which Christianity contributed most, but which was reinforced, to a far greater degree than is generally realised, by the clear and noble ideals of Hellenism, through the classical education received by the governing classes. It would be difficult to find any leaders of the age whose outlook on life was uninfluenced, if not formed, by one of these. In some, like Shaftesbury and Bright, Christianity was dominant; in others, like Mill and Morley, Hellenism; in Gladstone, Newman and Jowett the two streams met. But Christian ideals deeply influenced even those like Carlyle, George Eliot, Matthew Arnold and many others, who rejected Christianity. Indeed it was impossible to escape the influence of beliefs which filled the atmosphere and in which almost everyone was brought up. No country is ever permeated through and through by its religion; human nature is too varied, frail and rebellious, and its spiritual dress, even if it purports to be of a single material, is more or less stained and patched. The nineteenth century, like all ages, was polytheistic, but it had a less mixed crowd of deities than the twentieth, transferred its allegiance far less lightly, and as a whole it acknowledged, even where it did not profess, a great religion. The nation as a whole had a philosophy of life which might be called Christian; it had a common belief and common standard of conduct; and at the lowest it was governed by the ideal of respectability, the indispensable virtue of our fathers. The nineteenth century had a soul, a spirit: what soul, what spirit, has ours? The child of the Victorian age was born into a world of stable traditions and clear standards and was shaped from birth in their strong moulds. The child of to-day is born into a world whose traditions and standards are weakened, a world with inherited good habits, but no ruling philosophy of life. Through the last and still more the present century, the solid and impressive mansion which had been slowly built up through centuries of Christian belief, was steadily bombed.

Who dropped the bombs? Some would say, Science. But it would be more accurate to attribute the damage to the spirit of criticism which was at work long before, but in the twentieth century gathered momentum and threw off restraint. My own university education fell at the turn of the century and there is a strong contrast between the books read by my generation and by its successors. In my shelves, rows of books by Carlyle, Ruskin, Matthew Arnold, George Meredith, John Morley, Pater, Stevenson, Froude, date from my undergraduate days and indicate some of the influences, which, outside our ordinary studies, presumably formed my mind, and, I think, the minds of most of my contemporaries. Few of the present generation know much more than the names of any of them except perhaps Matthew Arnold and Stevenson, and, when I was a young tutor, they had already been replaced by Shaw, Wells, Arnold Bennett and Galsworthy, to whom, after the last war, was added Aldous Huxley, a profounder and more acute mind than any of them. I do not say that Carlyle and Ruskin were major prophets, but they were prophets. That word could not be applied to Shaw, or Aldous Huxley, or Galsworthy. For prophets have two marks. They must be critics; all the Victorian writers were that; Arnold and Ruskin were as critical of their age as any modern. But the positive element must outweigh the critical. Prophets criticise because they wish to reconstruct; the positive element in them far outweighs the negative; cynicism and flippancy are words they do not know; a vision of better things dominates their mind and drives them on; their denunciations spring from an intense faith; and behind the evils which they wish to destroy rises the vision of a new heaven and a new earth, the new Jerusalem descending from God out of heaven. None of these things can be said of the great sophists of the last forty years, men of lively minds, keen interest in ideas, and with the gift of expression, who were read by the large educated public. They are essentially critics who have destroyed with great success but have constructed nothing; not even H. G. Wells, a man of constructive instincts, an eighteenthcentury encyclopaedist, born out of due season.

Another contrast between the great Victorians and their successors is revealed in some words of George Meredith: 'I strive by study of humanity to represent it; not its morbid action. I have a tendency to do that, which I repress; for, in delineating it, there is no gain.... Much of my strength lies in painting morbid emotion and exceptional positions, but my conscience will not let me so waste my time.... My love is for epical subjects, not for cobwebs in a putrid corner; though I know the fascination of unravelling them.' The same sense of values to be preserved, of conscience in choice and treatment of a subject, appears in Kipling's *The Rabbi's Song* and in Thomas Hardy's *He resolves to say no more*. There is little trace of it in many writers of a later time, the Age without Standards, who have followed a precisely opposite principle.

A generation educated under these influences bears their mark, and is better trained for destroying an old world than for building a new one. There is no virtue in being uncritical; nor is it a habit to which the young are given. But criticism is only the burying beetle that gets rid of what is dead, and, since the world lives by creative and constructive forces, and not by negation and destruction, it is better to grow up in the company of prophets than of critics. There is a sonnet by Robert Bridges which has no title, but of which the real subject is education:

> Who builds a ship must first lay down the keel
> Of Health whereto the ribs of Mirth are wed:
> And knit, with beams and knees of Strength, a bed
> For decks of Purity, her floor and ceil.
> Upon her masts, Adventure, Pride and Zeal,
> To fortune's wind the sails of Purpose spread:
> And at the prow make figured Maidenhead
> O'erride the seas and answer to the wheel.
>
> And let him deep in memory's hold have stor'd
> Water of Helicon: and let him fit
> The needle that doth true with heaven accord:
> Then bid her crew, Love, Diligence and Wit
> With Justice, Courage, Temperance come aboard,
> And at her helm the master Reason sit.

Such vessels are not built in the shipyard of Messrs Shaw, Lytton Strachey, Aldous Huxley & Co.

The twentieth century was an age of demolition, in which only two forces were constructive. Commerce and Industry built up their great undertakings, as solid-seeming as the vast buildings which house them, and, like these, things of a day: Science laboured steadily at a more enduring creation: her palaces, firmly based, rise with steady growth to ever newer heights, and, like the giants of legend, her workers pile Ossa on Olympus and Pelion on Ossa, that men may climb to heaven:

"Οσσαν ἐπ' Οὐλύμπῳ μέμασαν θέμεν, αὐτὰρ ἐπ' "Οσσῃ
Πήλιον εἰνοσίφυλλον ἵν' οὐρανὸς ἄμβατος εἴη.

A magnificent and enduring work, and if science alone could save the world, her integrity, devotion and industry would save it. But pass from her kingdom to that of morals and religion, and you are in a waste land of shaken beliefs and shattered standards, where the house-breakers are still busy. Here the work of the twentieth century has been to destroy the settled convictions of the Victorian Age, and before their attack a solid, comfortable and in most ways noble view of life has crumbled.

No doubt some destructive work was inevitable. So long as there is life in the world, each generation will react against its predecessor, correct it, go beyond it. The house that accommodates the fathers never quite suits the children. But house-breakers rarely remember that the human race lives most happily in houses which each generation modifies to suit its own needs, keeping what is serviceable in the old building, and incorporating it in the new; certainly it cannot live on a bare site covered by untidy rubbish and relics of what has been overthrown. There is a parable in the New Testament, of a man from whom an unclean spirit was cast out, and who went through dry places seeking rest, but finding none took to himself seven other evil spirits worse than himself; and the last state of that man was worse than the first. That parable might have been written for us. The Victorian Age had its standards, its ends. The critics drove out its spirits—evil and good indiscriminately—and left the house empty, swept and garnished. Nature abhors a spiritual vacuum, and strange spirits occupied the vacant rooms—Nazism, Communism, Fascism, Pacifism—each demanding an exclusive worship, while those to whom these religions do not appeal are apt, like 'the democratic man', to admit a succession of guests, some of them disreputable.

So we stand to-day. There are items on both sides of the balance-sheet. On the debit side, there is the loss of standards, the loss of a definite philosophy of life, and the consequent loss of clear direction and steady drive. But there is a credit side too. Demolition was needed and the age of criticism has swept away some things which had to go and some which we are better without. We are less narrow, less prejudiced, more tolerant and humane than the weaker Victorians; we can apply to ourselves, as they could not, the words which Pericles uses of Athens and say: 'We give free play to all in our public life and carry the same spirit in our daily relations with each other; we have no black looks or angry words for our neighbour if he enjoys himself in his own way.'[1] Perhaps we have less cant, hypocrisy and vulgarity, though these spirits usually manage, unobserved, to find new reincarnations in each age. Our vitality is undiminished; this is not a worn-out world, and its vigour is not seen only in science and industry; it has created two new 'religions'—in Russia and Germany—since the last war. Finally, we have a large fund of inherited virtues. There is an enormous amount of goodness and goodwill and right feeling and action in the

[1] Thucydides, II, 37.

modern world. Take, as a single example, a virtue so common in this country that we hardly notice it, the unselfish public spirit which shows itself in unpaid public service and in money given or bequeathed for public purposes. When a real storm comes and we know ourselves in danger, we still have the ancient virtues of England at call: witness heroism by land, sea and air; in bombed cities, courage and cheerfulness and endurance, self-help and help of others; the traditional kindliness and decency of the ordinary English folk. These are great assets, not to be forgotten.

But in our satisfaction with our merits it is well to remember other less admirable sides of English life, of some of which I have spoken, and to reflect that we are living on character formed in the past by beliefs which are now shaken or destroyed. Character takes long to form, but it is not quickly destroyed. Lord Bryce was once asked: 'What do you think would be the effect of the disappearance of religious education from the schools?' 'I can't answer that', he replied, 'till three generations have passed.' We have inherited good habits, and habits persist almost indefinitely if there is nothing to destroy them. A plant may continue in apparent health for some time after its roots have been cut, yet its days are numbered. The case of Germany witnesses to the truth of this contention. Who, thirty years ago, would have believed a prophet who said that a decent, friendly, highly educated and civilised people, among whom Christianity was apparently still strong, would be capable of the persecution of the Jews, the horrors of the concentration camps, the barbarism, knowing neither justice nor mercy nor truth, shown in so many lands? How astonishing, we say, that such things could happen in the twentieth century! It is not in the least astonishing. The spiritual roots of Germany had been cut, and rootless virtues are precarious. But how strong are the roots of *our* virtues? The philosophy of life, the standards by which the Victorian and earlier ages were governed, have broken down. We are left with traditions and habits of conduct inherited from them, as the earth may for a time still receive light from an extinct star. But that light will not continue to shine, nor can these habits and traditions long survive the beliefs from which they grew. Those who reject Christian beliefs, cannot count on keeping Christian morals.

Some prophetic words of Plato, which might have been written for this age, indicate our problem. 'It is not', he says, 'the life of knowledge, not even if it included all the sciences, that creates happiness and well-being, but a single branch of knowledge—the science of good and evil. If you exclude this from the other branches, medicine will be equally able to give us health, and shoemaking shoes and weaving clothes. Seamanship will still save life at sea and strategy win battles. But without the knowledge of good and evil, the use and excellence of these sciences will be found to have failed us.'[1] Plato speaks the language of his own civilisation and talks of medicine, weaving, shoe-making and seamanship. To-day he would say that science, economics and sociology, industry and commerce will provide us with the frame of our society and satisfy its material needs, but that 'unless we have the knowledge of good and evil, their use and excellence will be found to have failed us'. It has been already 'found to have failed us'. Let us learn our lesson.

This generation then has a double task: to create the new order, of which we are always speaking; or, more accurately, to guide the nation through one of the great

[1] *Charmides*, 174.

social changes in its history; but also to train human beings fit to live in the new order, and, in Milton's words, 'to make in the towardly and pregnant soil of England a Nation of Prophets, of Sages and of Worthies'. New orders do not necessarily mean a great civilisation, nor do improved social conditions inevitably make better human beings. Inhabitants of a slum moved into a modern housing estate may carry their old habits with them and spoil their new surroundings; and we too may be unworthy tenants of an order however new and good. We have to transform a world with uncertain standards and vague values, with many virtues but no clear philosophy of life, into one which knows how to refuse evil and choose good, clear in its aims and therefore in its judgements and action. It will not be done merely by the extension of social services or the abolition of unemployment, important as these are, but by a change of mind and heart. That will not come of itself nor can it be left to chance. We must do what, in their different ways, Russia, Germany and Italy have done already; they have made great political and social changes, but they have not been content with these; they have trained men with a new outlook and a new way of life, conscious of an ideal which makes sacrifices pleasant and difficulties only a challenge to further effort. They have been concerned, after their fashion, with what Plato calls the science of good and evil, though their idea of good and evil may be very far from the true one. We have not: but unless we get a clear and right idea of good and evil, our new order will come to little, if it comes into being at all. It is a task for education in the widest sense, and needs first an educational system which will make it possible and next, within that system, an education which will achieve it.

CHAPTER II

CHARACTER AND ITS TRAINING

Standards; a philosophy of life; a principle by which to judge and rule it; a formula or formulas to integrate our civilisation, our new order; some knowledge of the 'science of good and evil'. How are these to be given? They are being given every moment—in cinemas, in advertisements, in newspapers and books and parliament and pulpit, through everything that we see, hear and read; and much of it is disintegration rather than integration. It is the more important that the greatest of all formative forces, education, should make its voice heard decisively above the babel of confused crying.

But are its accents clear and does it do what we need? It may do nothing, or do exactly the opposite and only add to our confusion. Listen to a description of modern education and its effects by the well-known American thinker, Mr Walter Lippmann:

There is an enormous vacuum where until a few decades ago there was the substance of education. And with what is that vacuum filled: it is filled with the elective, eclectic, the specialised, the accidental and incidental improvisations and spontaneous curiosities of teachers and students. There is no common faith, no common body of principle, no common moral and intellectual discipline. Yet the graduates of these modern schools are expected to form a civilised community. They are expected to govern themselves. They are expected to have a social conscience. They are expected to arrive by discussion at common purposes. When one realises that they have no common culture, is it astounding that they have no common purpose? That they worship false gods? That only in war do they unite? That in the fierce struggle for existence they are tearing Western society to pieces?...We have established a system of education in which we insist that while everyone must be educated, yet there is nothing in particular that an educated man should know.[1]

Mr Lippmann argues that American education creates 'no common culture, no common faith, no common body of principle, no common moral and intellectual discipline', and that it fails to do so because it is a congeries of subjects which are excellent in themselves but have no common purpose or have forgotten what it was. British education is less elective and eclectic, but much of this criticism seems to be true of it, its results and its present tendencies.

Our education has great virtues. It is fully conscious of part of its duty and performs that part as well as can be expected of any human institution. It imparts the knowledge generally considered desirable. It produces the specialists which a complicated society needs to maintain its machine. It teaches its pupils to use their intellects. Doubtless, it might do all these things better, but it makes good provision for them. We should be admirably educated if we had to be nothing but technical or professional machines, carrying out the routine of government, industry, commerce and other functions necessary to a material civilisation. Unfortunately, we have also to be human beings. We are concerned not only with livelihood but with the good life. And of this our education is only partly aware. Here and there it trains men for it, uncertainly, sporadically, fitfully; and the training depends on the

---

[1] Address to the American Association for the Advancement of Science, 29 December 1940, printed in *The American Scholar* (Spring, 1941).

insight of individual teachers and the almost accidental existence of certain schools.

This defect in education is reflected and illustrated in the state of Europe, whose industry, commerce, science, technology, medicine, are first-rate. It is a superb building, admirably equipped with the latest material improvements. Materially, it speaks a common language. Its learned men, its technologists, its soldiers and sailors, its doctors and teachers, its lawyers and administrators, use the same tongue, understand each other, are able and ready to co-operate in their various vocations. We are advanced, united, international, in our material civilisation; when we pass beyond it, Babel begins—in our relations with others and even within ourselves. We and our education have been too absorbed in the matter of life to think of its spirit. We must restore to it a vitamin, deficient both there and in our life—a religion, a philosophy of living, a definite ideal to guide, discipline and dominate the lives of individuals and, through them, national life. Education, that maid-of-all-work, has to set her hand to as many duties as a general servant. But two things she should give everybody before her work is complete—an intellectual attitude to life and a philosophy of life. I would define the right intellectual attitude as threefold: to find the world and life intensely interesting; to wish to see them as they are; to feel that truth, in Plato's words, is both permanent and beautiful. And a philosophy of life? The right intellectual attitude to life is already a partial philosophy of it. It is complete, if you extend it to cover Goodness, Truth and Beauty, and define Goodness to cover those words which have been trumpet-calls to many generations, and, once sounded by unknown men far back in history, have been borne round the world on the waves of the spiritual air, now loud, now low, but never wholly silent: love, justice, courage, self-mastery, mercy, liberty. Philosophy passes into religion when these are seen to point to and derive their validity from that ultimate spiritual reality which we call God. Philosophy and an intellectual attitude are high-sounding terms; yet their rudiments are within the powers of any school-child—to find work interesting, to see the difference between fact and fiction, and to acquire an outlook, a habit of mind, a sense of values, an insight into 'the science of good and evil', which will later ripen into a rational conviction. The fundamental task of education is to put into the mind some idea of what these things are, some desire to pursue them. An education that does this is a success: an education that does less is a failure. Our education seems to me to do it only partially and sporadically.

Consider the Certificate of General Education—and most children in secondary schools get no further—and ask what principle lies behind it, and you will probably conclude that if any principle integrates it, if any tie holds together its collection of loose sticks, it is an attempt to train some of the faculties and impart some of the knowledge which 'an educated person should possess'. Excellent so far; but this is not enough to produce 'a common faith, common culture, common body of principle'. From time to time reformers get busy. But they are more concerned with what the pupil must know and how his faculties should be trained, than with his sense of values and his knowledge of good and evil. And what he should know is interpreted in a utilitarian sense. Materialism continually besets education. Forty years ago it took a coarse form in the demand from a certain type of business man that secondary education should consist largely of book-keeping, typing, shorthand, and modern languages for commercial subjects. To-day our utilitarianism is more refined. All will be well, we are told, if we have more science, or more economics and sociology. And why not some American history, of which most of us are sadly ignorant? And now Russia is so important, more attention should be paid to Russian. And, when one comes to think of it, are we well prepared to deal with politics, knowing so little of other important countries, China, Japan, Latin America, and many, many others? Our ignorance of these things and much else is a grave handicap to living intelligently in a complicated world. But the remedy is not to crowd these subjects into an already overloaded school curriculum, or teach them to children, few of whom are interested in them, and none have the maturity of mind to grasp them properly. They are subjects for the adult, whose mind is mature and to whom they are practical and urgent problems, and there is no greater need than to give opportunities for their study through adult education. But that is not our method. Some country—let us call it Ruritania—rises above the political horizon, fills the newspapers and the public eye, becomes interesting and important for the moment. There is a general feeling that we do not know enough of Ruritania, and that something ought to be done about it. A public-spirited person, or an expert on Ruritania, writes to *The Times*. Teachers of Ruritanian point out how neglected the subject is in our schools and how few chairs of the Ruritanian language there are in the Universities, and urge that it should be included in the Higher Certificate syllabus and in language courses for a degree. The Board of Education is approached and blesses the project in guarded words. We all know this phenomenon: it occurs at least once a year. Generally—such is the force of human inertia and so many are the competing subjects—nothing is done. Ruritania passes out of the news and the agitation subsides into a few faint flickers at educational conferences. And that perhaps is fortunate. Otherwise another addition is made to an overcrowded curriculum, its chaos grows still more chaotic, still more devoid of system or plan; the shop-window is elaborately dressed but bears little relation to the goods in the shop; the face value of the currency is imposing, its purchasing power small. Such methods take us somewhere, but not where we need to go.

Our utilitarianism reveals itself in the discussion of the modern languages to be taught in schools—shall French, German, Russian, Spanish, Italian, have the first place? Various arguments are brought forward, difficulty, intellectual discipline, commercial value, help to international understanding, available texts and other relevant points. But one most important consideration is hardly ever mentioned—the quality of the literature in the languages concerned. And yet a major criterion in the choice of a language is the wisdom and greatness to which its knowledge opens the door, and obviously languages differ greatly in this respect; the little attention that we pay to it betrays our habit of mind. Here perhaps I may be allowed a personal memory. I was taught French and German at school: in French we read books of the quality of *Tartarin de Tarascon*, *Le Capitaine Pamphile*, *Le Roi des Montagnes* and *Monte Cristo*; in German after two terms on *Easy Passages for German Translation* we were thrown headlong into *Faust*, followed by Heine, Schiller and Lessing. Pedagogically, our German teacher's method was indefensible, educationally (in the highest sense of the word) it was right, that in a literature which has so little above the second rank we should have met its best writers and its one great genius. We learnt German, but also something more. Education would be the better if it had more of that spirit, and looked more steadily beyond material and immediate needs. Science, technology, economics, modern languages for commerce, are of course essential to the modern world. But their concern is with the means of life, not with its ends; and a clear view of ends is as essential to successful living as a mastery of means. We live—all of us—in two worlds; in the everyday world which changes in each age with the progress of material civilisation; and (whether we give it that name or not) in a spiritual world, without which Science could not believe in Truth, or Religion in God, or Good itself have any meaning. This is the world of values. To sacrifice it to science or economics or sociology or anything else is as fatal as to omit vitamins from the human diet. We do not pay enough attention to it.

I have suggested that our secondary education, while as efficient in its actual teaching as any human institution is likely to be, suffers in general from lack of integration, from the absence of a spirit to order and guide its processes, and that in the choice and teaching of subjects it thinks more of what its pupils should know than of their outlook on life. What of proposals for its integration? There are many, and we should soon be well if abundance of prescriptions were enough. Among them are education for freedom, for creativeness, for personality, for equality, for social change, for a dynamic society, for a world of science and technology. Dynamic, creative personality, equality, liberty, democracy, science, social change—these comforting words are often flung about, without any exact idea of what they mean or how far they take us. We ought indeed to be free, dynamic and creative, to develop our personalities; we live in a world of social change and science and should know how to do it. But do any of these proposals take us far? Will they solve, do they show any awareness of, our deepest problem? Are they more than skating on a surface below which are unplumbed and unregarded depths? Education for freedom: the value of freedom depends on how it is used. For creativeness. To create what? For personality. To develop what kind of person? For equality or an equalitarian life. Lived at what spiritual level? For the 'highly technicalised twentieth-century civilisation'. To understand techniques will not teach us to use them for good purposes. For social change. What is the soul of the new world to be? For a dynamic society. Dynamic for what ends? The Gadarene swine were very dynamic; so is Germany. We must go deeper than any of these prescriptions will take us. Excellent as they are within their limits, they will not reach our real disease. The prescribers have never asked what should be the guiding principle of the State, whose citizens they have to train; and, deeper still, what the individual is to be or to seek to be; they have never defined the good life for man. It is not enough to give people the knowledge necessary to live in a 'highly technicalised civilisation' or even the power of thinking clearly, unless they are given a clear conception of the kind of pattern they should weave, of the life which they and their fellow-citizens should lead. Without this they may be equipped with the means to realise their end, but they will be in the dark or in twilight about the end itself. Knowledge of science and technology and economics is not the end; nor are creativeness or freedom or even truth; they are indispensable to civilisation but too narrow a basis for it, and schemes that look no further leave us where we are—able to make and do almost all we want, but uncertain what we wish to make or do or be, ignorant of the fundamental 'science of good and evil'.

Anyone who looks at the present state of the world must feel that this is the problem of which we need to think most. But we shy away from it, partly through short-sightedness, partly through moral and intellectual cowardice. It is at any time the most difficult and dangerous of all problems, and doubly so to-day when the beliefs of Western civilisation are shaken. We know what to believe about science and modern languages and economics, or at any rate think that we can find out, or at worst that it does not so much matter if we make mistakes about them. So we succumb to the common and disastrous human instinct to run away from difficult decisions, and concentrate on freedom or creativeness or equality or technology, as if these, however important, were substitutes for something more fundamental. But the decision must be made: our own character and the character of our society depend on it: if we decide wrongly they will be bad, if we decide right they will be good; if we hesitate and haver, they will be impotent and at the mercy of any strong force.

But, it will be said, some of our education at least is 'integrated', and integrated round the very principle for which you are arguing, round standards and a definite view of life. Are we not always talking about character? Have we not always believed that it is more important than brains? Has not its development been the chief aim of English education, since Arnold defined his ideal as the training of Christian gentlemen? 'Christian', 'gentlemen' —what do these words connote except character and a philosophy of life built on this? And have we not been, in large measure, successful? Onlookers have a clearer view of the game than the players; and the feature which foreigners admire in English residential schools, and find wanting in their own, is the power of training character. Is not this the principle of integration which we want, and could there be a better?

I hesitate to introduce into my argument an institution

which excites lively passions; there is more objectivity in a bull looking at scarlet than in some critics contemplating residential schools. Yet it is a fact that the three most original British achievements in education are (in chronological order) the Residential School, the Workers' Educational Association and the Scout and Guide Movement. Other countries may equal or surpass our elementary, secondary, technical and university education; but these three products are creations of our own and are all known, admired and imitated abroad. Among these the residential school aims at producing, and on the whole does successfully produce, a definite type of human being with clear standards, and achieves more nearly what I have been pleading for than any other of our educational institutions. There are other schools which send their pupils out into the world with a definite attitude to life, but it is especially characteristic of the residential school to do it. Whether it likes it or not, it cannot help producing a common attitude to life among its pupils, not in virtue of its curriculum, which does not differ from that of the day school, but because it is residential. It has its pupils' whole time and their whole life, their hours of leisure as well as of work, for eight months of the year. In such circumstances a common ethos (which may leave room for great individual differences)[1] must develop automatically. The residential school cannot in its own interests neglect the character-training of its inmates or leave it wholly to the home. Nor can it neglect religion, at least in a country which sets store by religion. Hence the school chapel and religious worship and teaching and the development of a view of life. And, at its best, the residential school has

[1] Those who speak of the residential school as 'crushing individuality' may reflect that Sir Stafford Cripps, Mr D. N. Pritt and Sir Oswald Mosley were all educated at Winchester.

been and is admirably successful in producing men with right values and a clear view of life.

But it has not always been at its best, and then it has both succeeded and failed; succeeded in training certain moral qualities, and failed because our definition of character has been too narrow. Character means for us courage, truthfulness, trustworthiness, a sense of honour, independence, fair play, public spirit and leadership. These are national ideals and on the whole national virtues, and in developing them the English race and the English school compare favourably with any other. They are the qualities necessary if men wish to live together in a society, and the English insistence on them partly explains why we have so far been able to work passably well the most difficult form of society, democracy, in which there is a minimum of compulsion and a maximum of free co-operation. But these by themselves do not complete character. If a man has them, he should be able to 'withstand in the evil day, and having done all, to stand'. But life is wider and richer than the traditional virtues of the residential school. It includes art and thought and science, and all the capacities which create these and all the activities which they cover. Further, life is dynamic as well as static; it involves motion as well as standing and withstanding; and motion, if it is to be of any purpose, is towards a goal, rightly chosen and clearly seen. It is not enough to be able to do right, unless we know the right; and this knowledge is part of character. Here we are less successful. Indeed the history of mankind might be described by a cynic as a series of splendid expeditions towards the wrong goal or towards no goal at all, led by men who have all the gifts of leadership except a sense of direction, and every endowment for achieving their ends except the knowledge of ends worth achieving. We must not forget in our education this element, a sense of direction. We do forget it, if we are content that our schools should merely impart knowledge, develop and discipline the intelligence, train character in the narrow sense. They must also be places where the mind is enriched by the right visions and where the ends of life are learned.

The English find it difficult to take these aspects of school seriously. There is a common assumption among them that a boy good at games will be good in practical life, and that a boy good at books will not. Neither of these beliefs is borne out by facts or shared by any other nations except those of English blood. But Englishmen nurture in the depth of their hearts a feeling that intellectual interests are enervating. They do not really believe that the claim of Pericles for Athens—'Our intellectual interests involve no effeminacy'—could be true about anybody. They are better pleased with the ideal of the Spartans 'who from their cradle cultivate manliness by laborious discipline'.[1] The long roll of English statesmen and men of action from Raleigh and Chatham to Gladstone and Cromer, who have found inspiration, delight and consolation in literature, is nothing to them. They would have thought Wolfe incapable of taking Quebec if they had known his enthusiasm for Gray's *Elegy*, and been nervous about Charles James Fox's passion for Euripides, if his gambling debts had not suggested that he was a man of affairs. They would regard Napoleon's and Wellington's fondness for the *De Bello Gallico* as a dangerous symptom; as doubtless they would have disbelieved in Caesar's practical capacity, because he wrote a book on the theory of grammar during his Gallic campaigns, and quoted Menander when he crossed the Rubicon.

Hence the theory which is often heard at prize-days. Some distinguished general or admiral, some successful

[1] Thucydides, II, 39.

business man, returns for a few hours to the haunts of his youth and expounds his sentiments on the principles of education. They may be read in *The Times* any June or July, when English schools normally hold their prize-days. The speaker points out that it is not always the successful schoolboy who succeeds in after life. He himself was no good at work and never much cared for it; but then, he reminds his audience, it is not learning Latin and Greek that one looks for at school, but training of character and learning to play the game. How well one knows this doctrine! In any case it is superfluous. To preach it to schoolboys is carrying coals to Newcastle. Few of them need to be warned against over-valuing Latin and Greek, against a too arduous devotion to intellectual interests. But there is a graver objection to it. The doctrine is false. A character, trained in this limited sense, is admirable within its limits but inadequate to the needs of the modern world. It is deficient *as a character*. It may have, and at its best undoubtedly has, powers of leadership. But it is the leadership of a corporal or a sergeant. Such an education produces a superb army of N.C.O.'s; whereas the real business of the school is to train staff-officers, men able to face unexpected emergencies, to lead an army and not merely a platoon, to plan a campaign.

It would of course be grossly unfair to suppose that the residential school has always produced such limited types or produced nothing else. It was very different in Arnold's hands: he broadened the basis of education; whatever he taught—classics, history or scripture—he taught in its relation to life; he trained character, but he gave a philosophy of life to support it. And in this he has had many successors. Anyone who doubts this and supposes that residential schools turn out nothing but a regimented type without intellectual or other interests can refute his error by glancing through the pages of *Who's Who* or examining the names in any Cabinet and asking whether its members who were educated at residential schools compare unfavourably with those who were not. Still this has been the besetting danger of the residential school and the sharpest weapon of their critics. At their weakest they have sent out boys furnished with invaluable qualities of character but with character trained on too narrow lines; they have thought it enough to give them 'a habit of good behaviour without an intellectual basis'—the phrase is Plato's, who points out how inadequate an equipment this is for life in a disordered world. In this they have reflected the weaknesses of the nation itself, its Philistinism, its reluctance to think things out or to base conduct on principle.

What then shall we do?

Education is a vast continent and it will make for clearer thinking if we divide it into three main provinces, corresponding to the three main needs of human life. All men need to make a living—not a bare one, but the best that conditions allow. All men live in a society. All men have a personality to develop and the power of living ill or well. For all these education must provide, and it must therefore include a vocational element, a social or, as the Greeks would have called it, a political element, and a spiritual element. Men must learn to earn a living, to be good members of a society, to understand the meaning of the phrase 'the good life'; and education must help them to achieve these three ends. It must do this not for a limited class but for every citizen, though it will do it in different ways for different people.

The new society, then, like every society, will need three main kinds of education—vocational, social, spiritual. It must provide for its material existence and for the running of its machine, and the education dealing with this may be called vocational. It will need its technologists and skilled workers to feed it, clothe it and supply the necessities, comforts and even luxuries of life; its doctors, scientists, economists, teachers, administrators. So it will have every variety of technical education, and in its places of higher study it must provide not only for Medicine, Science and Applied Science, but for such subjects as Economics, Psychology, Sociology, Public and Colonial and Business Administration: the list can be completed by studying the Calendar of the London School of Economics. That, of course, is not to say that everyone will study all, or even any, of those subjects. In addition to training the numerous and various specialists which it requires, a society should give its educated members at least, not indeed specialist knowledge, but some perception of the general conditions and possibilities of modern civilisation, and a sense of the importance and uses of the techniques and specialisms essential to it.

Then our society will need social or political education, a training in citizenship, as we call it, which I leave to a later chapter, passing on to the third aspect of education —that which fits a man for living well. In practice it cannot be separated from the other two—education for a vocation and for citizenship—but in aim it differs from them. It has no name. You can call it the education of personality, but that word in turn needs definition, and it is simplest to take the old Greek analysis and think of it as the education of body, mind and character, to the highest degree of which each individual is capable. Of this immense subject I shall only touch on a side which, for want of a better word, may be called spiritual. The efficiency of a community will depend on its technical and vocational education, its cohesion and duration largely on its social or political education. But the quality of its civilisation depends on something else. It depends on its standards, its sense of values, its idea of what is first-rate and what is not. The vocational and the social aspects of education are essential, but the most fatal to omit is the spiritual aspect; fatal, because its absence may be long unperceived, and, as with an insidious disease, a State may suffer from it and be unconscious of its condition till the complaint has gone too far to cure. And this spiritual element is precisely what we tend to ignore. Yet nothing is more needed at the moment. The body of our civilisation risks destruction by war, and we are too distressed by that to notice that its soul is already more than half drowned in the turbid river of modern life.

During the last war the salvation of the world was assigned to science. Now we are disillusioned. Science, like medicine, is an integral part of civilised life. It is difficult for human beings to maintain health without doctors, but medicine is not health. It is difficult for a civilisation to be sound without science, but science is not civilisation, and few people can suppose that salvation is its business. To-day we tend to assign that role to psychology, economics and sociology. These branches of knowledge are indispensable to our civilisation. We have not enough of them. We need more. But though adjuncts and auxiliaries, they too are not saviours of society, and if we fix our hopes on them the year 1960 will find us so much further down the hill and looking for some other force to help us to recover our lost ground. Our knowledge of the sciences, natural or social, fixes the limits of the course within which the yachts on which humanity is embarked must sail, but does not indicate the goal of their voyage, still less supply wind to fill their sails.

The forces that move the world need to be informed

and disciplined by the intellect, but they are not in themselves intellectual. Is there any great event in history which does not bear out that truth? Economic or social conditions may prepare the way; the moving force is a vision. The ardour that created modern Germany and modern Russia came from a vision,[1] even if it was one seen through bloodshot eyes. An eternal trait of men is the need for vision and the readiness to follow it; and if men are not given the right vision, they will follow wandering fires. One tragedy of our world is that Hitler had a vision and his opponents had not. The weakness of England and of America is that (with plenty of science and a quantum at least of economics and sociology) they have seen no clear vision. Indistinct and blurred figures stir them in their uneasy sleep, but have not yet taken form. That has been a grave weakness in this war; it will be a much graver one, when we face the problems of peace.

If we are to cure it, we must look beyond (without overlooking) science, technology, economics, sociology, handicrafts, subjects 'with a vocational bias', and recall and extend a statement by Professor Whitehead that would probably surprise most English people: 'Moral education', he says, 'is impossible without—' What? Residential schools, games, a happy and disciplined family life? No, none of these. 'Moral education is impossible without the habitual vision of greatness.'[2] It could not be put more strongly—'*impossible*', '*habitual* vision' (not a chance and occasional glimpse). Outside Plato, there is no profounder saying about education.

A 'habitual vision of greatness' is necessary not only to moral education, but to all education. A teacher cannot give an adequate training in anything unless he knows,

[1] I do not mean to put the two visions on a level.
[2] *The Aims of Education*, p. 106.

and can make his pupil see, what is great and first-rate in it. How can you train a surgeon unless you show him the finest technique of surgery; or a teacher, unless he knows the best methods of educational practice; or an architect, unless he is familiar with the great examples of his art? So, too, with all subjects from building to farming, from carpentry to Greek prose. Much else may enter the student's training; but there is no stimulus like seeing the best work in the subject which he studies; he will have no standards, no conception of the goal to which he painfully struggles, unless he sees the best; he will slip insensibly to lower levels of ideal and practice, unless it is continually before his mind, unless, in fact, he has the 'habitual vision of greatness' to attract, direct and inspire. In all studies and in all spheres of life, knowledge of the best is essential to success. And if this is necessary in medicine and teaching and architecture and town-planning, must it not be necessary in character? And is not Whitehead right when he says that you cannot train character 'without the habitual vision of greatness'? Mere character training in the narrow sense could be carried out by a drill-sergeant; courage, endurance, fair-play, discipline, could be learnt on a parade ground, and the work would need a far less highly qualified staff than those of a school. There is something more to character training than this. It is common and disastrous to forget that the character must be trained through the intellect as well as by other means, and that part of the work of education is to enrich the vision of its pupils and thereby train their characters. A school that fails to do this is failing to do its work. That is a truth of which teachers and pupils cannot too often remind themselves. What more important service can school or university do for their pupils than show them the best things that have been done, thought and written in the world, and fix these in their minds as a standard and test to guide them in life? Men's achievements depend not only on the qualities of character (in the narrow sense) with which they tackle their task but also on knowing what is first-rate; ill-success in every field of life is due quite as much to ignorance of what is good as to incapacity to achieve it. One is apt to think of moral failure as due to weakness of character: more often it is due to an inadequate ideal. We detect in others, and occasionally in ourselves, the want of courage, of industry, of persistence which leads to defeat. But we do not notice the more subtle and disastrous weakness, that our standards are wrong, that we have never learnt what is good.

Take an example. The nineteenth century built cities of incredible ugliness, the twentieth century spoils the beauty of the country with hideous bungalows and defaces the beauty of Oxford by making it an industrial town—in perfect innocence but with disastrous results. It was not malice aforethought, it was pure ignorance. It was the absence of a standard. It was the failure to know what was really good. How essential then that the citizen should know and desire the best things—the best things in art and architecture, the best things in literature and thought, the best things in politics, industry and commerce, the best professional ideals, the best things in human character! In the perfectly educated community at least the leaders, and so far as possible their public, would have seen this vision not only in their own immediate work, but in many fields. They would know the best in imperial, national and municipal politics; in town-planning, housing, and the social services; in the earning and spending of money; in social and family relations; in thought and art, intellect and individual life. The more fields and the clearer the vision, the richer and greater national life would be.

School and university cannot do more than begin such a work; their pupils are too undeveloped, their time too short, to take in such a panorama. It must be begun at school, but it needs to be carried on and completed in later life and demands a provision for adult education which our shortsightedness has not yet dreamed of making. How inadequate is an education which fails to impart something of such visions! How misconceived is one which never makes the attempt! That is the disastrous flaw in the doctrine of those who suppose that a school has done its duty when it has taught pluck, self-reliance, truthfulness and the art of playing the game. These are indeed splendid qualities. But they are not enough to make a world. Achieve them and we shall still have achieved only a part of human virtue. The most indispensable viaticum for the journey of life is a store of adequate ideals, and these are acquired in a very simple way, by living with the best things in the world— the best pictures, the best buildings, the best social or political orders, the best human beings. The way to acquire a good taste in anything, from pictures to architecture, from literature to character, from wine to cigars, is always the same—be familiar with the best specimens of each.

Knowledge of the first-rate gives direction, purpose and drive: direction, because it shows what is good as well as what is bad; purpose, because it reveals an ideal to pursue; drive, because an ideal stirs to action. To have seen Oxford or Cambridge, Edinburgh or Bath makes a nineteenth-century industrial city and a drab or 'picturesque' suburb repulsive, or at least pricks the conscience and stirs a sense of something wrong. The sight of goodness in life or in literature or history gives a standard and a challenge. If anyone has been able to compare the first-rate with the second-rate, his criticism will not be merely bitter and barren, but creative, born of a vision perceiving the good, dominated by it and desiring to bring it to birth. 'The intelligence of every soul rejoices at beholding Reality, and once more gazing on Truth is replenished and made glad.'[1]

In the fable from which these words are quoted, Plato, describing how each human soul before birth drove across heaven in the company of the gods, and saw Beauty, Justice, Courage and the other virtues, says that success in life depends on how far, among the shadows, confusions and distractions of earth, the soul retains the memory of that vision. Plato's story is a parable of a good education.

Note. Dr F. H. Hayward's Books of 'School Celebrations' contain ingenious and attractive methods of introducing the pupil to great figures, moments and movements in history.

[1] Plato, *Phaedrus*, 247.

CHAPTER III

THE TRAINING OF CHARACTER THROUGH HISTORY AND LITERATURE

Our education then should not be satisfied with imparting the information which a pupil requires, equipping him for a vocation, teaching him how to use his mind. It should send him out with a definite spiritual attitude to life, and the material and basis for a definite philosophy of living. It should have the aim which it would probably profess to-day, which it would certainly not disclaim, but which in general it pursues half-heartedly and ineffectually, and in the university stage, especially in the newer universities, wholly abandons—the aim which education had 2300 years ago. Here is a description of the training of a Greek boy in the fifth century B.C.; consider, as you read it, if it would apply to our English education.

Education begins in the first years of childhood. As soon as the child can understand what is said, nurse and mother and the father himself exert themselves to make the child as good as possible, at each word and action teaching and showing that this is right and that wrong, this honourable and that dishonourable, this allowed by God and that not allowed. At a later stage they send him to teachers and tell them to attend to his conduct far more than to his reading and writing. And the teachers do so, and when the boy has learned his letters, they put into his hands the works of great poets, and make him read and learn them by heart, sitting on his bench at school. These are full of instruction and of tales and praises of famous men of old, and the aim is that the boy may admire and imitate and be eager to become like them. The music teachers, in the same way, take care that their young pupil learns self-control, and does nothing wrong, and when they have taught him to play, they teach him the poems of good lyric poets, and set these to music and make their harmonies and rhythms familiar to the children's souls, in order that they may become gentler and more rhythmical and harmonious and so fitted for speech and action. For the life of man in every part needs rhythm and harmony. Then they send the boy to the teacher of gymnastic, in order that the perfect body may serve the virtuous mind, and that he may not be compelled by physical defects to play the coward in war or in the other activities of life.[1]

Note here the aim—the overwhelming insistence on producing a definite type of character, a definite attitude to life. Education is conceived as spiritual training, and all its subjects, whatever else they are, are also food of the soul. That should be our model. Note too the methods; this steeping of the pupil in what is first-rate in 'tales and praises of famous men', in order that he may imitate them and wish to become like them; this discipline of the body, not for the body's sake but that the body may be the servant of the virtuous mind. That is the education which all human beings in all ages need.

It may seem a great narrowing of education; nothing about information or mental discipline; no word of science or economics; a restriction of it to training in goodness, to loving what is right and hating what is wrong. It is no doubt an excessive simplification, an over-concentration on one element; but for this age the emphasis is in the right place, nor does it in any way exclude other elements; it only stresses the supreme importance of character-

[1] *Protagoras*, 325f.

training. Such an ideal would not cause any upheaval in our education, or any serious recasting of the curriculum; it would only involve a change of attitude and emphasis in the teaching of certain subjects. Visions of greatness in human life and character are to our hand in two subjects taught in every school—literature and history, including the Bible, which is both literature and history.

Here then we shall find visions of the first-rate in human life and character. But to see them clearly, we must read literature and history in a particular way. There are many ways of reading both. Take history. Most of us treat it as a panorama, often broken and dim, in which are seen the adventures of man on the earth from earliest beginnings to the last syllable of recorded time. We read it vaguely, the mind caught by a dramatic scene, a striking character or event, an interesting fact: the kaleidoscope revolves, the combinations change, and, unless the memory is retentive, pattern and colours fade from the mind. Or, again, we read with purpose, focusing the mind on some special aspect; we concentrate perhaps on the discovery of particular facts, or the study of great movements, on the growth of civilisation or the rise and fall of peoples, on constitutional development or political thought, on nationalism or colonial expansion or social change. All these ways of studying are legitimate and necessary, but will not help us, except accidentally, in our present purpose. If we wish to find spiritual values and patterns of goodness in literature or history, we must look for them as deliberately as, if we were primarily interested in economics, we should note in our reading allusions to industry or trade or wages or anything that threw light on the working of economic forces. The study of history in schools changes. In my youth it is supposed to have stressed kings, generals and nobles, diplomacy and war; then it became fashionable to concentrate on social aspects and the life of the common people. It includes this and much more. But ultimately it is the story of the slow ascent of man from the animal to the savage, and from the savage to modern civilisation. In this story lie the deepest interest and most fruitful lessons, and here we can find what we are looking for. Many things have conditioned and contributed to the ascent of humanity; biology, climate, economics have played a part; but so have great men. Here we are on the track of the examples, the inspiration that we were seeking—on the track of the first-rate. It is on this side of history that we must concentrate if we are looking for standards and values and the first-rate in human nature and conduct. The record of peoples and civilisations and the growth and decline of institutions and nations offer no doubt visions of greatness; Greece was more than Pericles, Rome than Caesar, Britain than Cromwell or Chatham or Pitt. But it is in the personalities of history that we see most clearly courage and persistence, desire for wisdom and devotion to good—the great positive forces of the world by which humanity has climbed from cave and forest into a clearer air. Montaigne has written the motto for such a study of history: 'I would have the teacher remember the goal of his labours and be more concerned to impress on his pupil the characters of Hannibal and of Scipio than the date of the fall of Carthage.'[1]

Here certain distinctions are necessary. The makers of civilisation fall into three main classes—men of action, men of thought and knowledge, men of vision—a class which includes religious thinkers and teachers, poets and artists. These three classes make the rope by which men, with many halts and slips, climb slowly into a clearer air; all contribute to its strength: and seen from outside the

[1] Montaigne, *Essays*, I, 25.

three strands are combined so closely that it is hard to tell what each contributes or where they interlace. Some people suffer from colour-blindness, and can see only one strand. Thus early Christian fathers, like Tertullian, could not see the strand of thought and knowledge: thus in modern times Mr Wells sees little else, and in it sees chiefly the threads of science. But it is important to realise that the rope is of triple ply, and, so far as possible, to disentangle its components; we shall not understand civilisation if we forget any of the strands; we shall misunderstand it, if we do not clearly distinguish their contribution. It is difficult to exaggerate the influence of Faraday, Darwin and Pasteur, or, in a narrower field and for a shorter time, of men like Adam Smith; but their influence is wholly different from the influence of Socrates and Plato and the Stoics, of Christ, of St Augustine and St Thomas, or again from that of Alexander, Augustus, Charlemagne, Cromwell, Napoleon. No truism could be more obvious, but how often it has been forgotten! Each of the strands in turn is apt to seem, to those interested in it, to be the whole rope. In every age the strongest force fills the common eye and distorts the common judgement. In the past, religion was the offender, and the Church disregarded science or took the function of science into its own hands, and at various times decided that the earth was flat, that the Antipodes did not exist, that Hell was in the centre of the earth, and that the Creation took place some 6000 years ago. When religion restricted itself to its own function, the turn of science came, and popular imagination and some scientists made for the characteristic force of the age claims equally extravagant, unjustified and fallacious, and assigned it a dictatorship over life. As previously religion, so now science, like Bottom in Shakespeare, is to absorb every part in the drama: 'An I may hide my face, let me play Thisby too.' To-day, we are disillusioned but hardly wiser; for the pre-eminence allotted to science is being transferred to politics. Germany and Italy have looked for salvation to dictators, and we tend to think that the world will be saved by sociology and economics, by a managed currency or the organisation of international trade, by 'new orders' and 'planning'. Thus:

Opinion gilds, with varying rays,
These painted clouds that beautify our days:
Hope builds as fast as knowledge can destroy.

But the rope will not bear the weight of humanity if it has only one strand or even two. Science and politics are essential but they are not enough without the spiritual strand, which, using the word in the widest sense, we may call religion.

Therefore, in reading history as the record of human progress, education must see all three strands in the rope—spiritual, intellectual, political—study the men in whom they are embodied, and do justice to all. In fifth-century Athens it must remember Socrates and Democritus as well as Pericles; in the twelfth century A.D., St Bernard and John of Salisbury as well as Henry I and Frederick Barbarossa; in the sixteenth, Sir Thomas More and Copernicus as well as Henry VIII and Luther; in the nineteenth, Darwin and Shaftesbury as well as Bismarck and Cavour. We must judge these men in the light not only of their own age, but of all time, and estimate their contribution to civilisation *sub specie aeternitatis*, trying to read the writing of the Recording Angel and to divine the sentence of the Last Judgement. Here Time helps, and looking back we can discern the qualities that have brought mankind on, and those which have kept it back; the men and the nations who have deserted the army and dropped out of the struggle, and those who have been victorious or by their faith and endurance have made victory possible for others. Contemporary judgements are often reversed:

> O'er that wide plain, now wrapt in gloom,
> Where many a splendour finds its tomb,
> Many spent fames and fallen mights—
> The one or two immortal lights
> Rise slowly up into the sky
> To shine there everlastingly.

In the ascent of humanity, slow, devious and broken, Socrates is seen to matter more to the world than Pericles, St Bernard than Frederick, Sir Thomas More than Henry VIII, Pasteur and Darwin and, perhaps, Shaftesbury than Bismarck. Indeed in our survey we run the risk of undervaluing the men of action. They are an essential strand in the rope; and possibly a statesman who combines greatness with goodness, even if he contributes less to civilisation, deserves no less credit for his work than a great religious teacher or social reformer, or man of science; for his task, if it is rightly done, is even more difficult than theirs.

Having distinguished the three strands, political, scientific, spiritual, we can turn to look more closely at the great men, and learn what is first-rate in human nature by studying those who have embodied it. And here turning to what may be called the life of the spirit, we must again distinguish different types. There are men who have done in the spiritual world what Darwin and Pasteur did in the world of nature—revealed a new attitude and outlook, and so enabled mankind to live on levels which without their vision it could not have reached. These are the prophets and religious teachers, who with a few words make revolutions in the spiritual life of mankind; like the utterance of Hosea: 'I desire mercy and not sacrifice, and the knowledge of God more than burnt-offerings', or the words of Christ: 'Ye have heard that it hath been said, Thou shalt love thy neighbour and hate thine enemy. But I say unto you, Love your enemies, do good to them that hate you: that ye may be the children of your Father which is in heaven.' Such utterances change the world; higher levels of existence are revealed; a new life is conceived, even if it takes millennia to bring it to birth.

Then there are men to whom we owe a different revelation—that of goodness in action. Such, in one aspect of his life, was Socrates; such was St Bernard of Clairvaux, than whom few men are better worth study in difficult times, for he lived in an iron age.[1] In the world there was lawlessness and savagery, in the Church a corruption, to which our time, so critical of the 'failure of the Church', offers no parallel. It would have been natural if he had swum with the tide, or taken refuge from it in a hermitage or lapsed into pessimism and denunciation. Instead, patiently and resolutely, he threw himself into the desperate battle, turned the rout and made a better world possible. If there had not been many such men, saints canonised and uncanonised, famous and unknown, mankind would not have advanced:

> Their shoulders held the heavens suspended;
> They stood, and earth's foundations stay.

We can perhaps learn more from them than from the prophets, for their virtues are nearer to our capacities, if not to our needs.

Now turn from history to literature, the other great treasury of the first-rate in human nature and life. Here

[1] There is a good Life by Cotter Morison.

again, it is a question of angle of approach. In a work of prose or poetry we may be interested in date, sources, the biography of the writer, the contemporary or historical interest of his work; or in its technical aspects, in construction, metre, language; or we may read it for pure pleasure, indifferent to any other consideration; or we may study it deliberately as a vision of the world and of life. It is of this angle of approach that I wish to speak, and I would define it more exactly by saying that literature is a study, combined with delight, in the art of living, a vision of what is first-rate in human nature and life.

Literature, as a revelation of the first-rate in human nature and life, may take the form of direct exposition. Thus Matthew Arnold's *Morality* is a contrast between the spontaneous, effortless forces of Nature, and Morality, struggling and laborious, yet with a divine quality which Nature does not possess: thus Wordsworth's *Ode to Duty* is a balancing, almost a discussion, of two forms of goodness, the free, natural goodness,

> When love is an unerring light
> And joy its own security,

and one controlled and fortified by the law of duty; thus *The Character of the Happy Warrior* is a plain enumeration of the qualities which seemed to Wordsworth the best armour for the battle of life. These poems—and much of *The Prelude*—read almost like passages from Plato or Spinoza or Kant, or some philosophical or religious writer. In them poetry becomes deliberate criticism of life, unsystematic moral philosophy, written by men of imaginative genius (who are sometimes as good introductions to the subject as the philosophers). Such poems, like philosophy, are usually better appreciated and more enjoyed after the age of twenty than before it.

Then there are poems where the ideas are no longer abstract but clothed in a concrete form. In this class come works like Wordsworth's *Leech-Gatherer*, a story of a walk on a moor during which the poet met an old man gathering leeches in the ponds. None of his poems better illustrate the poet's power which he so modestly describes:

> In common things that round us lie
> Some random truths he can impart;
> The harvest of a quiet eye
> That broods and sleeps on his own heart;

in none has imaginative insight found more perfect poetic expression. It can be read almost without reference to the idea which it embodies and which the sub-title, '*Resolution and Independence*', records; but that idea dominated the poet's mind, even if a reader may not notice it.

Then again there are poems, like *The Faery Queen*, *Paradise Lost*, *Prometheus Unbound*, *The Idylls of the King*, in which a view of life is present, but latent. In all of them it is easy to forget or disregard the philosophy they embody, and, when the moral or idea in them loses its interest, the story may survive by its own vitality: as *Paradise Lost* has out-lived its theology without losing any of its greatness, and remains a masterpiece though it no longer justifies the ways of God to man.

In all these types of poetry a view of life is present, sub-merged in each at different depths. In *The Happy Warrior* it stands out and strikes the mind at once; in *The Leech-Gatherer* it may escape notice; in *The Faery Queen* or *The Idylls of the King* it must be looked for, if it is to be seen. Spenser, for instance, can be read for many reasons and looked at from many angles. We may be interested in his poetic development, in his vocabulary and versification, or in the vicissitudes of his stormy life; or we can lose ourselves in a world of romance, where, as on tapestry, knights and ladies, magicians and fairies move against a background of seas and palaces and

> Forests and enchantment drear
> Where more is meant than meets the ear.

But it is equally legitimate, and for our present purpose important, to be aware of another side of *The Faery Queen*. This is what a nineteenth-century critic, who looked for the view of life in *The Faery Queen*, found there:

The unity is one of character and its ideal. That character of the completed man, raised above what is poor and low, and governed by noble temper and pure principles, has in Spenser two conspicuous elements. In the first place, it is based on manliness. It is not merely courage, it is not merely energy, it is not merely strength. It is the quality of soul which frankly accepts the conditions in human life, of labour, of obedience, of effort, of unequal success; which does not quarrel with them or evade them, but takes for granted with unquestioning alacrity that man is called—by his call to high aims and destiny—to a continual struggle with difficulty, with pain, with evil, and makes it the point of honour not to be dismayed or wearied out by them. It is a cheerful and serious willingness for hard work and endurance, as being inevitable and very bearable necessities, together with even a pleasure in encountering trials which put a man on his mettle, an enjoyment of the contest and the risk, even in play. It is the quality which seizes on the paramount idea of duty, as something which leaves a man no choice; which despises and breaks through the inferior considerations and motives—trouble, uncertainty, doubt, curiosity—which hang about and impede duty; which is impatient with the idleness and childishness of a life of mere amusement, or mere looking on, of continued and self-satisfied levity, of vacillation, of clever and ingenious trifling.[1]

All this is undoubtedly present in *The Faery Queen* and it is possible both to enjoy the poem as poetry, and see and saturate oneself in the ideal which Dean Church found in it. And it is worth finding.

So far I have been speaking of poets, who had some moral in their minds and intended to convey a lesson. But the moralists are not necessarily the best moral teachers: the first-rate exists and is felt, even though no one calls attention to it. It is, as the Greek critic said of sublimity, an echo of greatness of mind, and when greatness is present, the waves of the air are stirred. The English are fortunate in having not only the greatest poet in the world, but one whose sense of good and evil is nearly unerring. Almost every type of character, and every interest of human beings, except religion and science, are to be found in Shakespeare. There is virtue and vice, greatness and pettiness, Claudius and Iachimo and Iago as well as Horatio and Imogen and Cordelia, Polonius and Osric as well as Kent and Paulina; but there is no doubt about the difference of good and evil. There is tragedy, down to those depths of gloom in which *Troilus and Cressida* was written; but in the darkness Shakespeare never forgot the existence of light, and by the side of characters like Pandarus and Helen and Ajax, whose worthlessness is more depressing than villainy, created the generous simplicity of Troilus and the wisdom of Ulysses. It is not a question of preaching morals about Shakespearian texts but of simply reading the plays in the spirit in which they were

[1] Church, *Spenser* (English Men of Letters), p. 151.

written. To see Lear and Gloucester, Edmund and Regan, Cordelia and Kent as their creator saw them is to share his vision of human good and evil, and to know what he thought first-rate; that in itself is a great education of character. Anyone steeped so deeply in Shakespeare as to absorb him can safely read Wycherley or *Don Juan*, if he wishes to read them. He will have a standard by which to choose and to reject.

The first-rate in human nature and conduct is present abundantly in history and literature, and we have only to look to see it there. But a further problem arises. Good and bad, corn and tares, grow indiscriminately in these fields. Attila, Caesar Borgia, Richelieu, Frederick the Great, Hitler are in a sense great men: Villon, Boccaccio, the Restoration dramatists are in their way first-rate: yet it is not this kind of excellence that we are seeking, nor should we exhibit as ideals of character and conduct Richelieu and Wolsey, or Heine, Stendhal and Byron, great though they are. Literature and history, like life itself, are a chaos of good and evil, and the evil is mixed with the good. Anyone plunged into this chaos runs great risks. At worst, he may be attracted, infected and corrupted by wrong or false ideals; at least he will be confused and drawn insensibly different ways, growing up with a dissociated personality which lacks unity of spiritual standards and values. The more sensitive and imaginative the character, the greater the danger. That is why Augustine, master of thought and passionate lover of poetry as he was, breaks out into a denunciation of education: 'Woe to thee, stream of human tradition! Who can resist thee? How long wilt thou sweep away the sons of Eve into that vast and stormy sea, which scarcely those who have embarked on the Cross can sail safely?' And

again: 'Who can unravel this twisted and tangled skein?
It is ugly: let me not look at it.'[1]

Our aim is to mould character on the principles of what
we have come to call Christian civilisation, achieving at
lowest the 'natural end of man—virtue and well-being in
community'.[2] We must see that we do it, and allow nothing
to hamper or defeat our purpose. That raises the difficulty
felt by Augustine and the question asked by Plato, which
puts the problem clearly and demands a frank answer.
'Youth is the time when the character is being moulded
and easily takes any impress one may wish to stamp on it.
Then shall we simply allow our children to listen to any
stories that anyone happens to make up and so receive into
their minds ideas often the very opposite of those we shall
think they ought to have when they are grown up?'[3] The
problem lies there. It is the biggest problem anyone concerned with education has to answer, for it deals with the
greatest task of education. One must not run away from
it or let it slip out of mind.

Shall we expurgate? Expurgation, in any but a limited
degree, is impossible. How can history be expurgated?
How can brilliant villainy and successful crime be ignored?
The difficulty is illustrated by the Bible, where cruelty
and love, truth and treachery, high religion and narrow
nationalism elbow each other; where the tricks of Jacob,
and the extermination of cities are bound in one volume
with the Sermon on the Mount; where the word 'blessed'
is applied to the merciful, to those who dash their enemies'
children against the stones and to Jael who treacherously
murdered a fugitive foe. How can such a book be expurgated? Anyone who tries to cut unchristian elements out

---

[1] *Confessions*, I, 16; II, 10 (tr. Bigg—mainly).
[2] T. S. Eliot.
[3] *Republic*, 377.

of the Old Testament will soon despair of his task.[1] And yet what dangers the Bible presents! How often during the ages the devil has cited scripture for his purpose and 'evil souls produced holy witness'! There is point in Oscar Wilde's remark: 'When I think of all the harm that book has done, I despair of ever writing anything to equal it.' The history of religion shows the disastrous effects of reading the Bible without discrimination, and treating the Beatitudes and Samuel's order to kill the Amalekites as if they were equally inspired. But history and literature are sometimes taught much as the Covenanters read the Bible,[2] and as little distinction drawn between the good and evil in them. We must distinguish, though we cannot expurgate.

History (for our present purpose) is a picture gallery, where we pause longest before the portraits of greatness, learning to distinguish the permanent stars of the human firmament from the meteors, no less brilliant for the moment, which flash across the sky and vanish, and not so dazzled as to confuse greatness with goodness. Between 1770 and 1870 three men changed the face of Europe and altered the course of history—Frederick the Great, Napoleon, and Bismarck. Most readers are dazzled by their genius and achievements and ignore the perhaps more permanent result of their lives—that they impressed on the plastic mind of man a false ideal. Who can measure its corrupting and destructive power? Greatness does not excuse vice or crime, but it enlarges their influence; 'If the light that is in thee be darkness, how great is that darkness.' If there is any truth in the Christian conception of life, if civilisation consists in the advance of justice, mercy and truth, in substituting co-operation for struggle,

[1] It has, however, been done admirably for the Psalms in *A School Psalter*, by R. B. Henderson.
[2] Cp. the picture of the Covenanters in *Old Mortality*.

and a growing sense of the meaning of man's duty to his neighbour, it would have been better for the world if these three great men had never been born; Europe has paid and is paying for their lives in rivers of blood. Their political achievements are well described in Augustine's words: *Remota iustitia quid sunt regna nisi magna latrocinia?* 'Banish justice and what are empires but large-scale brigandage?' We can hold this view without becoming quietists, pacifists or anarchists. Political power, empires, statesmen and statesmanship, are not incompatible with justice, as the career of another great man shows, whose life falls within the same period, Abraham Lincoln; or that of President Masaryk, who worked in a smaller field but deserves to be ranked with Lincoln as the ideal democratic statesman. Both are associated with political struggle, and with four years of war. We can measure the gulf separating Lincoln from Frederick the Great and Bismarck—a gulf as wide as that between heaven and hell—by the famous words of the Second Inaugural:

The Almighty has His own purposes. 'Woe unto the world because of offenses! for it must needs be that offenses come; but woe to that man by whom the offense cometh.' If we shall suppose that American slavery is one of those offenses, which, in the providence of God, must needs come, but which, having continued through His appointed time, He now wills to remove, and that He gives to both North and South this terrible war, as the woe due to those by whom the offense came, shall we discern therein any departure from those divine attributes which the believers in a living God always ascribe to Him? Fondly do we hope—fervently do we pray—that this mighty scourge of war may speedily pass away. Yet, if God wills that it continue until all the wealth piled by the bondman's two hundred and fifty years of unrequited toil shall be sunk, and until every drop of blood drawn with the lash shall be paid with another drawn with the sword, as was said three thousand years ago, so still it must be said, 'The judgements of the Lord are true and righteous altogether.'

With malice toward none; with charity for all; with firmness in the right, as God gives us to see the right, let us strive on to finish the work we are in; to bind up the nation's wounds, to care for him who shall have borne the battle, and for his widow, and his orphan—to do all which may achieve and cherish a just and lasting peace among ourselves, and with all nations.

Let us then study Frederick, Napoleon and Bismarck, recognise their greatness to the full, and appreciate whatever is good in them and their work, but let us place by their side men like Lincoln and Masaryk, and mark the contrast. If we are told that moral judgements are out of place in the study of history, we can shelter ourselves behind the authority of the greatest of recent English historians, who, well aware of another view, wrote:

The weight of opinion is against me when I exhort you never to debase the moral currency or to lower the standard of rectitude, but to try others by the final maxim that governs your own lives, and to suffer no man and no cause to escape the undying penalty which history has the power to inflict on wrong. The plea in extenuation of guilt and mitigation of punishment is perpetual. At every step we are met by arguments which go to excuse, to palliate, to confound right and wrong, and reduce the just man to the level of the reprobate....So that we have no common code; our moral notions are always fluid; and you must consider the times, the class from which men sprang, the surrounding influences, the masters in their schools, the preachers in their pulpits, the movement they obscurely obeyed, and so on, until responsibility is merged in numbers, and not a culprit is left for execution.

A murderer was no criminal if he followed local custom, if neighbours approved, if he was encouraged by official advisers or prompted by just authority, if he acted for the reason of state or the pure love of religion, or if he sheltered himself behind the complicity of the law. The depression of morality was flagrant; but the motives were those which have enabled us to contemplate with distressing complacency the secret of unhallowed lives.[1]

Unless we follow Acton's maxim, unless we judge, unless we clearly distinguish greatness from goodness, history has as much power to corrupt as to instruct; it ceases to be an instrument of moral education.

That is true of literature also. There, too, flowers and weeds grow together and some of the flowers are bright but poisonous. It is easier to expurgate literature than history, and almost everyone would agree to some amount of expurgation. Nobody puts into a child's hands books condemned by the law as obscene, nor even every page of the great writers of the world. But there are obvious dangers in expurgation, and they have been put clearly by Cardinal Newman in a lecture to a Catholic University which is one of the best discussions on the subject. He is talking of university education; but *mutatis mutandis* his words apply to schools:

If Literature is to be made a study of human nature, you cannot have a Christian Literature. It is a contradiction in terms to attempt a sinless Literature of sinful men. You may gather together something very great and high, something higher than any Literature ever was; and when you have done so, you will find that it is not Literature at all. You will have simply left the delineation of man, as such, and have substituted for it, as far as you have had anything to substitute, that of man, as he is or

[1] Acton, *The Study of History*.

might be, under certain special advantages. Give up the study of man, as such, if so it must be; but say you do so. Do not say you are studying him, his history, his mind and his heart, when you are studying something else. Man is a being of genius, passion, intellect, conscience, power. He exercises these various gifts in various ways, in great deeds, in great thoughts, in heroic acts, in hateful crimes....Such is man: put him aside, keep him before you; but, whatever you do, do not take him for what he is not, for something more divine and sacred.[1]

Literature, then, ceases to be a portrait of man, if everything that falls below Christian standards is eliminated from it; and further, so treated, its study ceases to be a preparation for the life into which its pupils go.

We cannot possibly keep them from plunging into the world, with all its ways and principles and maxims, when their time comes; but we can prepare them against what is inevitable; and it is not the way to learn to swim in troubled waters, never to have gone into them. Proscribe (I do not merely say particular authors, particular works, particular passages) but Secular Literature as such; cut out from your class books all broad manifestations of the natural man; and those manifestations are waiting for your pupil's benefit at the very doors of your lecture room in living and breathing substance. They will meet him there in all the charm of novelty, and all the fascination of genius or of amiableness. To-day a pupil, to-morrow a member of the great world: to-day confined to the Lives of the Saints, to-morrow thrown upon Babel;—thrown on Babel, without the honest indulgence of wit and humour and imagination ever permitted to him, without any fastidiousness of taste wrought into him, without any rule given him for discriminating 'the precious from the vile', beauty from sin, the truth from the sophistry of nature,

[1] *The Scope and Nature of University Education*, Chap. 8.

what is innocent from what is poison. You have refused him the masters of human thought, who would in some sense have educated him because of their incidental corruption. You have shut up from him those whose thoughts strike home to our hearts, whose words are proverbs, whose names are indigenous to all the world, the standard of their mother tongue, and the pride and boast of their countrymen, Homer, Ariosto, Cervantes, Shakespeare, because the old Adam smelt rank in them; and for what have you reserved him? You have given him 'a liberty unto' the multitudinous blasphemy of his day; you have made him free of its newspapers, its reviews, its magazines, its novels, its controversial pamphlets, of its Parliamentary debates, its law proceedings, its platform speeches, its songs, its drama, its theatre, of its enveloping, stifling atmosphere of death.[1]

Ruthless expurgation is a moral danger.

To expurgate literature is as impossible as to exterminate microbes, but we can take the same measures against its corruptions as we take against microbes. Some of the worst can be destroyed or avoided; we can make people aware of the existence and character of others; and we can immunise human beings from their attack by building up the general health, till it is strong enough to resist infection. 'The mischief', as Newman says, 'is to be met not with argument, not by protests and warnings, but by means of the great counterfascination of purity and truth.' Bring people up in the company of the first-rate, whether in art, thought, morals, or anything else and they will instinctively detect what is inferior. Anyone used to good pictures, good wine, good literature or good men, is not likely to care for bad pictures, bad wine, bad literature or bad men, and needs no further protection than the standard insensibly implanted by living with the first-rate.

[1] *Ib.*

Reading the poetry of Aeschylus, says a character in Browning, has somehow spoilt my taste for twitterings; and provided that it does not make them conceited or inhuman, men need to have their taste spoilt for twitterings, and most of all in the things that are most important.

Naturally we read contemporary literature, which mirrors the interests, movements and problems of the day, is easily intelligible, and may include writers destined for immortality. But to read nothing else is to have no standards of comparison, to be narrow and provincial, to risk confusing the ephemeral with the eternal, the cry of the day with the music of the spheres. I saw recently a course of lectures on Housman, Galsworthy, Shaw, Somerset Maugham, James Joyce and others, advertised under the title 'Some authors worth reading'. In one sense the description was justified; all these writers are able craftsmen and in different ways documents on their time. But an equally descriptive title would have been 'Some authors not worth reading'; no one would learn from any of them what, in the full sense of the words, goodness and greatness are. That is one use of reading 'the classics', Greek, Latin or more recent. They give perspective and proportion to our view of our own times; they have a quality of which 'the world is impatient; it chafes against it, rails at it, insults it, hates it; it ends by receiving its influence and undergoing its law. This quality at last inexorably corrects the world's blunders, and procures that the popular poet shall not finally pass for a Pindar, nor the popular historian for a Tacitus, nor the popular preacher for a Bossuet' (Matthew Arnold). These are delusions from which it is better to be free.

If then we are needing literature to give the vision of what is spiritually first-rate, to form character, and moral standards, we must select what is first-rate in these fields and reject what is not. Some writers are good for our purpose and others are bad, others neutral. If we are looking for the first-rate in ideals and conduct, we shall choose Isaiah, not the Book of Judges; Virgil, not Ovid; Shakespeare, not Marlowe; Milton, not Congreve; Johnson, not Sterne; Shelley, not Byron; George Meredith, not George Moore; Robert Bridges, not A. E. Housman. Even among those writers we admit, we shall make a further selection, preferring those—such as Aeschylus and Plato, Shakespeare and Dante—who, of all Europeans, have seen farthest and reached highest and best reveal the greatness of human nature. Then our pupils will see the first-rate and learn the difference between *quod semper, quod ubique, quod ab omnibus*, and *quod aliquando, quod alicubi, quod a nonnullis*.

'What!' you may say, 'Are we not to read Congreve or *Don Juan* or A. E. Housman, or any other writers whom you put on an arbitrary *Index expurgatorius*? Plato, Shakespeare and Dante, by all means, but why not the others too? They have, in their different degrees, literary power, beauty, genius; and some of them are already ranked among the immortals by the secure verdict of time.'

Yes, certainly let us read them, but let us realise what we are reading and why. Poetry may be great, yet barren of the highest things in human nature and life. Literary and spiritual excellence are separate things and the one may exist without the other. But, as in history we are dazzled by greatness, so in literature we are dazzled by genius. Greatness in a statesman, genius in a poet are realities with a value of their own and it is perverse to deny their reality and value, but it is equally perverse to let them blind us to the presence of spiritual and moral littleness. Unless either moral goodness, nobility of mind, spiritual greatness are mere words, or literature has no concern with life, writers, like statesmen, should be judged separately, on both counts.

This may sound a platitude, yet in fact we often fail to make the distinction and read unaware of what we are reading. Take, for instance, two popular authors of the last fifty years, Edward Fitzgerald and A. E. Housman. Fitzgerald's *Omar Khayyam* was a favourite with the last generation and read with whole-hearted admiration by many persons who would have been horrified by his view of life, had not their minds been lulled by the sonorous words into unconsciousness of the meaning:

> We are no other than a moving row
> Of magic Shadow-shapes that come and go
>   Round with the Sun-illumined Lantern held
> In Midnight by the Master of the Show;
>
> But helpless Pieces of the Game he plays
> Upon this Chequer-board of Nights and Days....
>
> O Thou, who Man of baser Earth didst make,
> And even with Paradise devise the Snake:
>   For all the Sin wherewith the face of Man
> Is blackened—Man's forgiveness give—and take.

How many orthodox Christians have read those lines, fascinated by their stately movement and music and quite unaware of their gloomy determinism, their indictment of theism!

In this generation the place of Fitzgerald has been taken by A. E. Housman, who has in a higher degree the same qualities of music of words and mastery of form, and a pessimism more self-centred, more self-pitying, with a touch of abjectness which is remote from the dignity and self-restraint of the Victorian writer. Some readers of Housman are probably unaware of his meaning—otherwise his Collected Poems would not be among the books at a School Prize-Day—and more have not fully realised the implications of his view of life. They are too fascinated by his poetry, as poetry, to attend to what he is saying. But that is not true of all his readers, as the experience of an English lecturer in Japan shows:

I thought A. E. Housman would be a good English poet to read. The English is very clear, and it is all a bit gloomy, so I thought they would like it all right. And I like it very much myself, so I thought I'd be able to put it over.... I think Housman would have been a good deal shocked by what they made of him. In fact, I am not sure that Housman might not have felt ashamed of himself if he had read those little essays. Because he does literally say what they thought he did, when you come to look at it.... This is what one of them wrote down, almost literally, and most of them took the same line: 'I think Housman is quite right. We will do no good to anyone by dying for our country, but we will be admired and we all want to be admired, and anyway we are better dead.'[1]

The naïve Japanese were no doubt far more ignorant of Housman than their teacher, but they understood him better; and we should imitate them.

The story may also serve to remind us that we can be poisoned by other things than an overdose of sex. Actually our literature has been less sex-ridden than that of some other countries; the puritanism of the English tradition and perhaps a natural sanity and balance in the English mind have saved us till recently from losing a sense of proportion and allowing a fraction of life to seem its greater part; still more from confusing lust with love. But 'sexual respectability, however important, is not the whole and final concern of life',[2] and literature can be pernicious

[1] *Listener*, 1 January 1942.
[2] Sampson, *Concise Cambridge History of English Literature*, p. 504.

without being immoral or obscene. The cynicism of *Don Juan* is as ignoble and injurious as any immorality in the poem; the morals of Burns were not much better than Byron's, but his generosity of spirit and sense of goodness are a liberal education; while many writers, who would pass the most censorious censor, can corrupt the mind by their attitude to life.

The same problem—that of choosing one's company—must be faced in literature as in life; it has similar implications and should lead to similar results. 'Will you gossip with your chambermaid or your stable-boy, when you may talk with kings and queens?' There are attractions in the company of stable-boys; they have their own special range of experience and knowledge, and may even be more entertaining and less embarrassing associates than royalty. So, too, with literature. A poet may be a genius, an artist, a master of music and language, and at the same time he may be worthless as a man, or the atmosphere in which he lives may be unhealthy or poisonous. We may read him for his other qualities; though a stable-boy as a man, he may be a king as a writer; but we should realise when he is a stable-boy, and when he is a king. I do not suggest that we should refuse to read writers of modern or ancient times, in whom genius or talent is united with a view of life which we reject; still less that we should read bad poets or writers, because their morals are sound—spiritual excellence does not turn bad poetry into good. I only urge that we should distinguish art and morals, greatness as a poet and greatness as a man; that in reading literature we should be quite clear why we are reading it. Is it for the language or the music, or for the thought? Is it the technique, or the revelation of life that attracts us: beauty, desired because it is beauty and no more, or a beauty in which the highest ranges of human thought and action are revealed? In literature, as in other things, it is possible both to admire and to condemn: and, if we are to have standards in life as well as in art, both are necessary.

Let me sum up. I began by saying that if we are to have a new world, we need human beings to make and live in it, and that we must not leave their education to chance. In the past, men accepted the Christian ideal even if they did not live the Christian life; a child born in the nineteenth century had its mind formed unconsciously by the atmosphere and beliefs around it. There is no such definite formative influence to-day and we must find one. I suggested that education could help to do this, if it showed its pupils the first-rate in life and character as they are revealed in history and literature. All Englishmen should have what Plato wished for his ruling class:

We would not have our Guardians grow up among representations of moral deformity, as in some foul pasture where, day after day, feeding on every poisonous weed they would, little by little, gather insensibly a mass of corruption in their very souls. Rather we must seek out those craftsmen whose instinct guides them to whatsoever is lovely and gracious; so that our young men, dwelling in a wholesome climate, may drink in good from every quarter, whence, like a breeze bearing health from happy regions, some influence from noble works constantly falls upon eye and ear from childhood upward, and imperceptibly draws them into sympathy and harmony with the beauty of reason, whose impress they take.[1]

[1] *Republic*, 401, tr. Cornford.

CHAPTER IV

FROM ATMOSPHERE TO REASON

Our fundamental need and a chief task of education to-day is to form the right attitude to life and to give what our age lacks, clear values and definite standards. In childhood this must be in the form of an instinctive attitude to life, but not a philosophy of it; an attitude that comes from living with what is first-rate, and so acquiring a sense of it, a love for it, an instinctive repugnance to its opposite. That is as much as can be done in earlier years, as, long ago, Plato saw: 'As for wisdom and firm, true belief, a man is fortunate if he acquires them in advancing years; to possess them with all their attendant blessings is to have reached the full stature of man. But by education I mean goodness in the form in which it is first acquired by a child. If pleasure and pain, liking and dislike, are formed in the soul on right lines before the age of understanding is reached, and if, when that age is attained, these feelings are in concord with reason, thanks to early discipline in the right habits—then this concord, regarded as a whole, is virtue. But if you consider one factor in it, the rightly disciplined attitude to pleasures and pains, by which a man from first to last hates what he should hate and loves what he should love—if you isolate this factor and call it education, you will be giving it its true name.'[1]

A definite philosophy comes late (Plato thinks 'in advancing years'). Goodness indeed must be acquired by children but acquired in non-rational form, as a habit of feeling pleasure and pain at the right things, hating what

[1] *Laws*, 653.

should be hated and loving what should be loved. This right feeling comes from early training in the right habits; and this training is the essence of early education—Plato reserves the word education for it; but as people grow up and learn to use their reason, the grounds for these habits are seen and a rational philosophy develops which justifies, explains and fortifies them. It is important that it should develop, for though without the right habits there will be no philosophy or the wrong one, without the philosophy even the best habits are insecure. Atmosphere is transitory, attitudes can change, habits may lose their hold, and none of them have the strength of a rational conviction about life. 'True opinions', as Plato said, 'are a fine thing and their results altogether good, so long as they stay with us; only they will not stay long, but run away out of the human soul, and so they are of little value, unless one fastens them by the tie of cause.'[1] Or, as one might say, an opinion based merely on habit has a shallow foundation which needs to be driven deeper into the firm rock of reason. The vision of goodness in history and literature nourishes goodness in the soul; but the ideals which these subjects contain are at best unsystematic and though they imply a view of life, they do not define or state it, and an education confined to them 'sets up culture in the place of Religion and leaves Religion to be laid waste by the anarchy of feeling'.[2] So in the later years at school the pupil should be at least introduced to a rational philosophy of life. But what philosophy?

A critic may have already asked on what principle certain men and authors were selected in the last chapter as patterns of the first-rate in human ideals and conduct. Why Socrates, St Bernard, Sir Thomas More, Shaftesbury, Lincoln, Masaryk, rather than Frederick the Great, Napo-

[1] *Meno*, 97f. [2] T. S. Eliot, *Selected Essays*, p. 384.

leon and Bismarck? Why Aeschylus, Plato, Dante, Shakespeare, Shelley, Wordsworth, Robert Bridges, rather than
Villon, Marlowe, Congreve, Sterne, Byron, Heine, Stendhal, Housman? It is not a question of mere greatness—if
so, the choice, at least in some cases, might have been
different—but of what is first-rate in ideals and conduct.
And on this latter score, why this selection? On what
general principle is it based?

I might reply that it is based on the principle of *quod
semper, quod ubique, quod ab omnibus*, that all ages and
universal assent would regard most of these men as masters
in the art of living. They have outsoared the shadow of our
night, and shine beyond question permanent stars of the
human firmament. The science, the politics, the commercial
and industrial systems, the social life of the age of Aeschylus
or Plato or Dante or Shakespeare have passed away and
become matters of antiquarian interest, but the writings of
these men, mere words, preserved on the most fragile of
materials, have survived, as fresh and living as on the day
when they were written down. They meet some permanent
need not only of their own epoch but of all time, and in a
world of change and death possess the secret of immortality.
Securus judicat orbis; the judgement of the world is hard to
challenge, and its judgement on Plato, Dante, Shakespeare
and even on Shelley and Wordsworth, is not likely to change.

Is there any common element in these writers, any
philosophy discernible in their writings? One's first instinct would be to say 'no'; they are so different, they
come from such different peoples, times and civilisations;
and most of them are not systematic thinkers or philosophers in the current sense of the word. Yet, whatever
their differences, they belong to one family, a strain with
strongly stamped characters, which no one could confuse
with the other great civilisations of the world, Indian or

Chinese: and if we ask what stamped these characters on them, there is only one reply—Greece, Rome, Palestine. Our civilisation, spiritual and intellectual, was born in Greece; Rome applied Greek thought to the life and institutions of a great empire; Christianity added new forces which modified and developed its Graeco-Roman inheritance. We are not Greeks, Romans or Jews, but our air is charged with influences from Greece, Rome and Palestine. However ignorant we may be of them, they will mould us. However we may react from them, we bear their marks. A man may know nothing of Greek thought and literature; he may be an agnostic or an atheist; but Greece, Rome and Christianity have made Western Civilisation, permeate its thought, morals, literature and institutions, and touch its members at every moment of their lives. It is as well, for they are the oxygen in its atmosphere and if they disappeared from it, its life would cease. It is characteristic of the weakness of our education, that most people know nothing of Greece and an increasing number know little of Judaism or Christianity.

The genius of Western civilisation is summed up completely and briefly in the lines:

> Think on the seed ye spring from! Ye were made
> Not to live life of brute beasts of the field,
> But follow virtue and knowledge unafraid.[1]

In the name of this double ideal the Ulysses of Dante calls on his men to venture on the unknown Atlantic; it inspired Bishop Foxe in founding Corpus Christi College, Oxford, in 1516, and appears in the preamble to his Statutes as the aim of higher education:

We have no abiding city here, but we seek one to come in heaven, at which we hope to arrive with the greater ease

[1] *Inferno*, XXVI. 118 (Laurence Binyon's translation).

185

and despatch, if while we travel in this life, we rear a ladder whereby we may gain a readier ascent. We give the name of virtue to the right side of the ladder, and that of knowledge to the left....

The words reveal their origin; ἀρετή and ἐπιστήμη inspired the life and thought of Ancient Greece, passed thence into the vocabulary of Europe, and gave our civilisation the double but indivisible ideal of virtue and knowledge. The word virtue was continually reinterpreted: but we recognise *idées mères* of our own civilisation in the cardinal virtues of Plato—Wisdom, Courage, Temperance and Justice, and in the longer list of Aristotle which adds to these Intelligence, Moral Insight, Liberality, Munificence, High-Mindedness, Right Ambition, Good Temper, Friendliness, Truth, Just Resentment, Modesty. Christianity, in the Beatitudes and elsewhere in the New Testament, but most of all in the life of its Founder, modified and added to, but did not supersede this vision of human goodness, a composite yet harmonious ideal which inspires and pervades Western civilisation and gives it amid all its differences a certain unity of direction. Therefore, in education, to form the growing mind and character, we shall choose writers and men who are most permeated by this ideal and in whom it appears at its purest and greatest, not those in whom it is diluted or distorted or who are in rebellion or reaction against it; Lincoln and Masaryk, not Napoleon or Bismarck or Hitler; Plato, Dante, Shakespeare, Shelley, Wordsworth, not Marlowe, Sterne, Byron, Heine. Here is the main stream of the river, here is the current which leads to the sea, and here the boats of youth must be launched, not in back-eddies and side-streams.

I have now implicitly answered the question asked above—to what philosophy our education should lead, when we pass from atmosphere to a reasoned view of life, and floating influences and impressions crystallise into a rational conviction. It will be the philosophy which lies behind that atmosphere and those influences. If Greek thought and Christianity created the soul of Western civilisation, formed its mind and are the vitamins in its life-blood, then these are the philosophies for which we are looking, and before his education is completed everyone should have an idea what they are. Many people never realise the connection between them; some even oppose them to each other. But in history and in Christian thought the two are linked indissolubly. Christianity surviving from the downfall of the ancient world salved and adapted Roman organisation and Greek thought, and incorporated both in the new house that it built for Western civilisation. The West owes to Greece the conclusions about God and conduct which the human mind reached without revelation and which we call natural religion and natural morals (is there any nobler or more concise expression of the latter than Plato's words 'Goodness is the health, beauty and well-being of the soul; evil is its disease, deformity and weakness').[1] A knowledge of these should enter into any scheme of higher education, so that people can enter life with a reasoned philosophy of it and not merely with good habits.

Some people may wonder why I suggest that the best introduction to natural religion and morals is through Greek thought, and that every educated person should have an acquaintance with it. The answer is partly given in some words of T. H. Green. From Socrates and his followers

comes the connected scheme of virtues and duties within which the educated conscience of Christendom still moves,

[1] *Republic*, 444.

when it is impartially reflecting on what ought to be done.... The articulated scheme of what the virtues and duties are, in their difference and in their unity, remains for us now in its main outlines what the Greek philosophers left it.... Once for all they conceived and expressed the conception of a free or pure morality, as resting on what we may venture to call a disinterested interest in the good; of the several virtues as so many applications of that interest to the main relations of social life; of the good itself not as anything external to the capacities virtuously exercised in its pursuit, but as their full realisation.... When we come to ask ourselves what are the essential forms in which, however otherwise modified, the will for true good (which is the will to be good) must appear, our answer follows the outlines of the Greek classification of the virtues. It is the will to know what is true, to make what is beautiful; to endure pain and fear, to resist the allurements of pleasure (i.e. to be brave and temperate), if not, as the Greek would have said, in the service of the state, yet in the interest of some form of human society; to take for oneself, to give to others, of those things which admit of being given and taken, not what one is inclined to but what is due.[1]

Not only did the Greeks create the theory of natural morals, but their exposition of it has certain advantages over any other. They produced, in the *Republic* of Plato and the *Ethics* of Aristotle, two text-books on morals, which are unlike other text-books in being written by men of genius. Further, they have a simplicity and directness which belong to pioneers and are impossible to a later age. 'The Greeks', said Nietzsche, 'are simple, like genius; that is why they are the immortal teachers.' No one begins to study the geography of a district on a six-inches-to-the-mile map; he starts with one of smaller scale, which shows main

---

[1] *Prolegomena to Ethics*, § 249 f.

features in clear relief and omits confusing detail. It is equally foolish to commence the study of morals or politics either on large maps of them or on inferior small ones. In every subject the most exhaustive book is the worst for the beginner; and if he is sensible, he chooses one which will fix in his mind essential points and main problems, before he proceeds to complications and refinements. Because they are such books, the *Republic*, the *Ethics* and the *Politics* are incomparable introductions to moral and political questions.

If I were asked what knowledge of Greek thought might reasonably be given in the later school years, I would suggest that the pupil should at least be introduced, if possible to Aristotle, and certainly to Socrates, Plato and the Stoics and to the conception of *areté*, which runs like a gold thread through the achievement of Greece. There is no equivalent for the word *areté* in English, though there is plenty of the thing in English life. It is 'virtue' not in the modern but in the old sense of the word; 'excellence' with no moral sense necessarily attaching to it. Everything, the Greeks said, has a use, a function, a virtue of which it is capable. Take things as different as a knife, an eye, a doctor. Each of them has a use and is capable of a virtue. A knife's use is to cut, an eye's to see, a doctor's to keep or make us well; and their virtue is achieved when they fulfil their use and function. If they do this, we call them good, if they fail, they are bad—as knives, eyes, doctors. Hence, the task and problem of each of them is to fulfil its function and so achieve its virtue. It is an argument in which it is difficult to see a flaw.

But what is true of knives and eyes, is true, the Greeks thought, of men also. They too must have a function, a use, a virtue of which they are capable and which it is their business to achieve; and in so far as they achieve it, we shall call them good. It is easier to see the function and virtue of an eye or a knife than of a man: and in fact he has many functions, and therefore many virtues to strive after. A human being is a member of a family—a son or a daughter, husband or wife, father or mother; he is a citizen, a member of a state; he has a profession or occupation; in each of these roles he has a different function, and in each function is capable of a virtue, an excellence, which consists in doing the particular job well, in being a good son or daughter, a good citizen, good in his occupation—whether it is that of Prime Minister or of shop assistant. He, no less than the knife or the eye, is judged by the way in which, in each particular capacity, he does the job in question well. But that is not enough. Man is more than a citizen, a parent or child, a person with an occupation; he is also a human being and in that capacity, too, is capable of a virtue. As a human being he has a body, an intellect and a character, and his business is to make the most of each of these, and see that all three are developed to the excellence of which they are capable, used rightly and used to the full. He must aim at *areté*, at virtue, in all.

This was the clue which the Greeks followed through the labyrinth of life. Its business, they thought, is to seek the highest and make the most of whatever a man is or does. They admired every kind of virtue, of excellence, sought after them and tried to create a society in which they could be achieved: and this ideal, this purpose partly explains why in so many fields of life they achieved an excellence which, long after they have perished, remains a model and an inspiration.

There may be better ends, but this is not a mean one, and it is simple, intelligible, convincing and practical. It leaves money in the right place. It is a perpetual challenge in hours of doubt, weariness, slackness, pessimism. It is a philosophy consistent with Christianity; only, where

Plato and Aristotle thought, not unplausibly, that the Reason was the noblest thing in man, and the highest life, therefore, the life of the Reason as lived by poets, artists, philosophers and men of science, St Paul has a different conception of the highest virtue, and has expounded his view of human excellence in the 13th chapter of the first Epistle to the Corinthians. The Greek ideal may seem too impersonal to English minds. Yet among all peoples it is the motive force in the creative artist, who seeks perfection for its own sake through language, or paint, or stone, or sound: and outside the ranks of artists, many people are driven on by it to do in their special field the best work of which they are capable. In it there is something, which lies at the heart of all morals, the passionate desire for good, simply because it is good.[1]

The ideal of *areté* is a moral philosophy in itself, and this conception of excellence as something to be sought in every sphere and activity is a valuable corrective to our narrower idea of virtue. Apart from it, every educated person ought to have some knowledge of certain individual Greek thinkers. Socrates, Plato, Aristotle, and Epictetus and Marcus Aurelius among the Stoics, are the most important for our purpose, in themselves and because of their influence on the world, and every pupil after the age of seventeen, who is capable of receiving it, should be given some idea of them; of Socrates for the example of his life and the stimulus and intellectual discipline of his thought, of Plato, because he is not only one of the great religious thinkers of the world but also in the direct line that leads to Christianity. 'Every problem which Plato discusses is still alive to-day.'[2]

[1] For a further account of *areté* see *Greek Ideals and Modern Life*, by Sir R. Livingstone, p. 69f.

[2] Whitehead, *Adventures of Ideas*, p. 15. There is no more stimulating and instructive book on Western civilisation.

Aristotle is more difficult. His influence on human thought has been enormous, though different from Plato's. In morals and in politics, as in natural history, his approach to a subject is scientific and inductive. But his gritty style and prosy manner are not attractive, and though there are many translations of his *Ethics* (some extremely bad), there is as yet none with notes for English readers.[1] Still the *Ethics* is one of the great books of the world: it propounds a clear, rational, noble view of the art of living; and it is fascinating and stimulating to take his list of the separate virtues, and his detailed account of each, and compare these with our own views on the subject, seeing where we should agree or differ, where we have gone beyond Aristotle, and where we can learn from him.[2]

But, it will be said, do you expect everyone to learn Greek, and are you not adding an enormous subject to an overcrowded curriculum? The answer to both these questions is 'No'. For anyone interested in literature and language to be ignorant of Greek is a great loss, but obviously only a small number of persons will learn it. But the others can easily make the acquaintance of Greek thought in the translations. Nor does the programme suggested here demand much time; though it contains nourishment for a life-time, its bulk is small. There is no question of an elaborate study of Plato, still less of the Stoics, whose moral thought alone concerns us. Half-a-dozen books on the shelves of the school library and effective encouragement to read them, in or out of school hours, open the door to a great world.[3]

[1] Mr Rackham's translations (one in the Loeb Series, one published by Basil Blackwell) are excellent.

[2] Books III. c. 6 to IV fin. These books and x. 6 to end are of most interest to the ordinary reader.

[3] For Socrates and Plato, the World's Classics *Selections from Plato, The Republic*, translated and edited by Professor Cornford, *Portrait of Socrates*, by

In history and in thought Greece leads on to Christianity, and the teaching of this in schools raises the so-called problem of religious teaching. It is not too much to say that the spiritual future of this country depends on its right solution and on the solution being carried rightly into practice. In the last nineteen centuries Christianity has been the greatest new fact in the history of Europe, which is unintelligible without some knowledge of it. It meets us in every stage and phase of our civilisation since the first century A.D., in politics and social life, in thought, literature, art, music, architecture. You may think it a deplorable incident in the development of man, but to anyone ignorant of it Western civilisation is a tapestry from which half the pattern has been cut out. Incidentally, its 'book' is both the finest monument of the English language and the greatest book in the world. Thus, quite apart from any religious reasons, some knowledge of Christianity must be given in education.

That raises the question what should be taught. Religious education is not a question of knowing the dates and authorship of the books of the Bible, or the meaning of phrases like 'the abomination of desolation', but of seeing Christianity as a way of living, as a life that was actually lived. This should lead to a knowledge of the Christian theory of life. The Life leads to the Creed. So it was in the history of Christianity, where the Creed was a late growth, a belief to which the actual experience of Christians led, and which embodied that experience but did not precede it: the Nicene Creed was formulated 300 years after Christ's death; the Apostle's Creed is not earlier than the middle

Sir R. Livingstone: for the Stoics, any good translation of Epictetus such as that in Oxford Classical Translations, and Marcus Aurelius in the same series. The above books on Plato are recommended because they have an introduction and notes for English readers; reading translations of Plato which give no such guidance is apt to be unprofitable.

of the second century and received its final formulation much later.[1] The individual should travel by the same road as the early Christian community: he should arrive at the Creed, not start from it; and it will mean infinitely more to him, if he comes to it, as the early Christians did, as a rational account of facts which he knows and of an experience which he has had. That indeed is the road by which most, if not all, people do travel: they come to accept the Creed because after living and thinking it seems to them the most rational account of the facts of history and of their own experience; they may, of course, learn it at any age or stage but so learnt it is inert knowledge; only personal experience will bring it to life. That is the regular process and right method in all education—first practice, then theory; first the facts, then the formulation of a principle to explain them: 'education is the drawing and directing of youth towards that right reason which the law affirms and the experience of the eldest and best has affirmed to be right.'[2]

This is not to say that we can at any stage dispense with dogma. Some dogma is inevitable. To say that the teaching of Jesus, or any of it, conveys the truth about life, is a highly dogmatic statement, implying a very definite view about the universe and human nature; to say that the teaching is false or valueless is equally dogmatic; and it is also dogmatic to say that we cannot form an opinion on the matter but must suspend our judgement. Agnosticism, like theism or atheism, is dogmatic and there is no credit, least of all any intellectual credit, in halting between two opinions, when in fact you must *act* as if one or the other was true. Only a people with the English indifference to

---

[1] Probably the early Christian recited the Creed only once in his life, at his Baptism.

[2] Plato, *Laws*, 659.

logic could have originated and approved an attempt to find an intellectual excuse for not making up the mind in matters where action is inevitable, and where any action implies a theory of conduct. Agnosticism enables English intellectuals conscientiously to indulge in the national vice of keeping thought and action apart, and concealing from the right hand what the left hand does.

How much dogma should be taught at school? The following suggestion by Professor L. A. Reid of Newcastle is worth consideration:

There is one (and only one) living God, the Author and Sustainer of the universe, whose nature is wisdom and love. Whilst the existence and nature of God can be apprehended in many ways (e.g. through thought in philosophy and scientific activity, or experience of beauty in nature and in art, through friendship and community of every kind and through suffering and joy), the Christian believes the nature and love of God to have been as completely embodied and revealed as it is possible for it to be revealed in a single human being, in the person, teaching, life and death of Christ. Not through his teaching alone (Christianity can never be reduced to a code of ethics) but through the quality of his life itself and in the manner of his death the Christian believes to be shown the very nature of God, of self-sacrificing love. The true and only true way of man's life he believes to be founded upon humble submission and confession before God. The Christian believes that only through the apprehension of the love of God and in freely given submission to His will can he properly understand the love of brother-man, and the Brotherhood of Man becomes a reflection of the Fatherhood of God. Christianity is humanistic but not merely humanistic. It believes that the sanctity and the equality of human beings are not *ultimately* human attributes but are derived from the purpose of God. And finally, this view of life is one which views ultimate reality not as material, but as spiritual and in some sense eternal.

Such a statement is of course very incomplete, and of course it would not be taught in this abstract form to children. It is a sort of 'jumping-off ground' for further thought and experience. It is a minimum, and as far as possible it avoids speculations. It asserts, for example, that the nature of God is revealed in Christ, but it does not attempt to formulate *how*.

It may be added that, whereas the Creed is composed of historical and theological affirmations, which do not explicitly demand any particular conduct though no doubt they imply it, this statement stresses Christianity as a gospel of action and points definitely to the kind of action which it requires. That is an advantage; for Christianity is too often regarded, both by those who profess it and those who reject it, as an intellectual belief and not as a way of life; in teaching it is important to stress the latter aspect.

On some of these points there may be disagreement, but there can be no doubt that higher education is incomplete without some knowledge of Hellenism and of Christianity (to put these in their chronological order). If we were Indians or Chinese, it might be otherwise; but our origin and traditions are different; we can learn from the East but we belong to the civilisation of the West and shall neither understand nor master it, if we are ignorant of the rock from which we are hewn. Without some knowledge of Hellenism and Christianity men go into the world having, at best, a partial and inadequate view of human greatness and goodness, and lacking a clear idea how life should be lived. With it, we shall have met men at their highest and we shall know the two great European interpretations of the nature and destiny of man. The spirit, design and aim of Western civilisation will become clear, and we can follow it with intelligence, and some hope of success.

I quoted earlier[1] Mr Lippmann's criticism of American education, which describes a condition to which we are tending, if indeed we have not already reached it. The following passage from his lecture is equally worth our consideration:

It is said that since the invention of the steam engine we live in a new era, an era so radically different from all preceding ages that the cultural tradition is no longer relevant, is in fact misleading. I submit to you that this is a rationalisation, that this is a pretended reason for the educational void which we now call education. The real reason, I venture to suggest, is that we reject the religious and classical heritage, first, because to master it requires more effort than we are willing to compel ourselves to make, and, second, because it creates issues that are too deep and too contentious to be faced with equanimity. We have abolished the old curriculum because we are afraid of it, afraid to face any longer in a modern democratic society the severe discipline and the deep, disconcerting issues of the nature of the universe, and of man's place in it and of his destiny.... Modern education has renounced the idea that the pupil must learn to understand himself, his fellow men and the world in which he is to live as bound together in an order which transcends his immediate needs and his present desires. As a result the modern school has become bound to conceive the world as a place where the child, when he grows up, must compete with other individuals in a struggle for existence. And so the education of his reason and of his will must be designed primarily to facilitate his career. By separating education from the classical-religious tradition the school cannot train the pupil to look upon himself as an inviolable person because he is made in the image of

[1] P. 135f.

God. These very words, though they are the noblest words in our language, now sound archaic. The school cannot look upon society as a brotherhood arising out of a conviction that men are made in a common image. The teacher has no subject matter that even pretends to deal with the elementary and universal issues of human destiny. The graduate of the modern school knows only by accident and by hearsay whatever wisdom mankind has come to in regard to the nature of men and their destiny.... The emancipated democracies have renounced the idea that the purpose of education is to transmit Western culture. Thus there is a cultural vacuum, and this cultural vacuum was bound to produce, in fact it has produced, progressive disorder. For the more men have become separated from the spiritual heritage which binds them together, the more has education become egoist, careerist, specialist and asocial.

These words accurately diagnose the disease of Western civilisation and suggest its cure.

'But', someone may object, 'these are the methods of Hitler. Your ideal may lead in a different direction, but it has the same character. You wish to form the childish mind, when it is powerless to resist, to impose a view of life on it, to ignore its right to freedom. You will destroy the plant, so rare, delicate and precious in the human garden —the desire to see things as they are and so follow the argument where it leads. And in the end your fate will be the nemesis of dictatorship—death of intellectual integrity and of anything that can be called intellectual life.' No doubt there is a danger here but there is sufficient latitude even in the individuals and authors suggested for study in the previous chapter (who are in any case only specimens taken from a much longer available list of suitable models) to avoid any risk of narrow outlook. Aeschylus, Plato,

Virgil, Dante, Shakespeare, Milton, Goethe, Shelley, Wordsworth have indeed something common in their fundamental attitude to life, but a mind formed by their study is not likely to be one-sided or blind. There would be more justice in the criticism that a standard derived from them would be a Least Common Multiple, so vague that no one would be offended by it but no one helped.

But when a critic speaks of the danger in forming the growing mind, I am inclined to ask him: 'And you, do you not impose a view of life on your child? Do you allow him to grow up dirty in person and habits, greedy, cruel, a liar, an egotist living for himself? Do you say to him: some people think that might is right and that the strong should take what they can and the weak suffer what they must; others think that life is a quest for pleasure and that the wise man evades any duty to his state or his neighbour and tries to live tranquil and undisturbed with his friends; make up your mind on these points, I express no opinion about them? Do you bring him up to believe that there is no distinction between right and wrong? But if so, are you not arbitrarily deciding the biggest of all questions? When you come to history, do you leave your child to suppose that Hitler is as good a model as Abraham Lincoln, that burning heretics is a sound method of propagating religion, that in the Industrial Revolution the champions of laissez-faire may have been right and their opponents wrong? Judgements on these points are more than a condemnation of persons and facts; they imply and rest on a definite view of life.' The fact is that the firmest believer in freedom moulds, or, if we prefer the phrase, tyrannises over, the mind of his child and takes liberty from it in the cradle.

It is fortunate that most people do try to implant a view of life in their children, for if they do not teach, the world does. Every film and newspaper and novel teaches. Every advertisement page, every platform on the Underground Railway preaches a sermon on the Virtue of Acquisitiveness. 'Here', they say, 'are goods necessary to your happiness, beer, motor-cars, whisky, cigarettes, permanent waves, "collars for discerning men". All can be bought for money; if you have money, they are yours—collars, whiskies, motor-cars, permanent waves.' The advertisers have no qualms in enforcing their doctrine, no objectivity, no respect for delicate consciences, no interest or scruple about effects on character. They have something to sell and mean to sell it, and though they may not believe in Latin, their motto has been written in words of Horace which describe and denounce a Roman weakness:

Rem facias, rem;
Si possis, recte; si non, quocunque modo rem:
'Make money, money; rightly, if you can; if not, by any
means, money.'[1]

This hoarse clamour drowns the low voices of right values, reason, even of commonsense; the more important to make those voices ring in the ears of youth. Even so they may grow faint in later life.

For we exaggerate the power of teaching to fix the human mind unalterably. Jesuits may have claimed to be able to do it in the first seven years of life; yet not all their pupils have died good Catholics. Recent psychology has talked in the same strain, but the latest pronouncement on a subject is not the same thing as the last word on it. Facts point another way. Do children brought up well in good homes always grow into good men; have none of us discarded views in which as children we were carefully indoctrinated? Personally, I was brought up in a conservative

[1] *Epistles*, I. 1, 65.

atmosphere and regarded Gladstone as an incarnation of evil; to-day, I am a liberal, and should look to the future more happily if I saw a modern Gladstone among our politicians. Most people have similar experiences. Liberty has outlived many tyrannies, and human nature, or rather human reason, has a way of asserting itself; *expellas furca, tamen usque recurret*; and perhaps the most constant law of human conduct is that extremes always produce reaction. The discipline of the Mediaeval Church is followed by the license of the Renaissance, the rule of the Saints by the Restoration Drama, the Classicism of the eighteenth century by the Romantic Revival, the photographic art of the nineteenth century by Surrealism and Cubism. The contemporaires of Tennyson could see no defects in him, their successors no merits. In one age human beings walk on the right side of the road; in the next they will be found in the ditch on the left. The one thing, alas! which they cannot do is to keep in the centre. And the danger, such as it is, of dominating a pupil's mind becomes negligible when the teacher is aware of it, believes in truth and has a respect for human personality; as he must if he has any respect either for Hellenism or for Christianity.

In the past totalitarianism and tyranny might conceivably have suppressed permanently any views but their own. In fact, they have not done so. The invention of printing, while it has given dictators new weapons of great immediate effect, has enormously reduced their ultimate power. The Emperor Domitian was wise when, having executed the republican leaders, he destroyed their writings. 'His savagery attacked not only the authors but even their books, and the triumvirs were assigned the duty of burning in the Forum these memorials of illustrious talent. Presumably Domitian thought that those flames destroyed the voice of the Roman people, the freedom of the Senate, the moral consciousness of mankind; he went on to expel from Rome the teachers of philosophy and drove into exile all liberal teaching, to prevent any trace of goodness meeting his eyes.'[1] Domitian's attempt to exterminate adverse thought might have succeeded before printing existed. It failed; to-day it would be hopeless. Literature—in the first century A.D. a small river—has grown, partly through the natural additions to it, partly through its dissemination by printing, into a vast ocean where all the thoughts which have crossed the mind of man through three millennia can be found, swimming on the surface or easily dredged up from the depths. Here, in countless forms, are conservatism, liberalism, communism, anarchy; atheism, agnosticism, religion in its many forms; every system of morals, every view of life or of the state. This ocean is round us and no one can hold the human spirit back from sounding in its depths—the human spirit, unquiet and curious, and grown still more so, since the day when Eve made her decision and accepted the serpent's offer; 'your eyes shall be opened, and ye shall be as gods, knowing good and evil'.

But it is as important to distinguish good and evil as to know them: and, at least for educated persons in the democratic countries, this is the real problem. Our danger is not too few but too many opinions; not to be penned in a single belief but to be puzzled by innumerable alternatives; not a closed mind but an irresolute one; to drift unanchored from one station to another, from deeps to shallows, from safe water to the rocks; an incapacity to refuse the evil and choose the good. A major task of education is to help to the right choice.

[1] *Agricola*, 2.

CHAPTER V

TWO DRAGONS IN THE ROAD

Standards, right values, the science of good and evil—to implant these is an essential part of education. Many forces thwart this work, but two of the most serious hindrances to it are examinations and specialisation.

The examination system is both an opiate and a poison. It is an opiate because it lulls us into believing that all is well when most is ill. 'Look', the public says, 'at this list of scholarships; see how many children have got their G.E. Certificate: something is clearly happening; the school is doing its job.' Something no doubt is happening; but it may not be education: it may be the administration of a poison which paralyses or at least slows down the natural activities of the healthy mind. The healthy human being, finding himself a creature of unknown capacities in an unknown world, wants to learn what the world is like, and what he should be and do in it. To help him in answering these questions is the one and only purpose of education. But that is not the prime aim of the ordinary pupil who is working for a G.E. or Higher Certificate or for a scholarship or a degree, and for whom the examination becomes much more important than seeing 'visions of greatness', and 'getting through' excuses all shortcomings and disguises all omissions. I am speaking here throughout of external examinations, not of those set by the school, as tests of progress, which are useful and necessary. Examinations are harmless when the examinee is indifferent to their result, but as soon as they matter, they begin to distort his attitude to education and to conceal its purpose. The more depends on them, the worse their effect. For disinterested-ness is the essence of all good education, and liberal educa-tion is impossible without it.

It is not suggested that nothing is learnt and no educa-tion received in working for an examination; that would be obviously untrue. But, to recur to my previous meta-phor, the examination system is a poison which slows down education in most cases and in some paralyses it, and no one wholly escapes its bad effects. The slow or stupid child suffers most, since preparing for the ordeal occupies more of its time and mind; and for some intelligent but nervous children examinations become an obsession. But the keenest student knows the sense of relief when he finishes his last examination and feels himself free to read and study what interests him simply because it is interesting, without any thought of what he is 'expected to know' or 'what may be set'. The blinkers are gone; he can look round with unrestricted eyes; and he knows how the young Athenian felt who answered Socrates' question whether they should pursue a certain intellectual inquiry: 'Should we, do you say? Are there any pleasures worth living for like these?'[1]

It is not only the pupil but—and this is far more serious —the teacher, who finds his energies and attention drawn from education to examination needs. No doubt there are schools and teachers which resist the insidious pressure, teach their subject for its interest and for nothing else and burn no incense on the examination altar. But the pres-sure is hard. Most people judge a school by its examina-tion results. Its reputation, however well-established, is affected by them; and a school with a name to make or competitors to face has an overpowering temptation to commend itself to the world by obtaining as many Scholar-

[1] *Phaedrus*, 258.

ships and G.E. and Higher Certificates as possible. Such results are intelligible to Boards of Governors and to the general public, and are generally expected by them. The teacher is tempted to show his competence by securing a big list of awards, the headmaster is tempted to demand them in the interest of the school:

> Things done, that took the eye and had the price,
>> O'er which, from level stand,
>> The low world laid its hand
> Found straightway to its mind, could value in a trice.

And, apart from this, however idealistic headmaster or teacher may be, they must reflect that a pupil's future in life may depend on an examination result and that their duty is to see that he is successful.

Any evils that might follow from the disappearance of examinations are nothing to the harm they do. They are in fact a refined form of the old and now universally condemned system of 'payment by results'; but whereas under it the payment was a money grant to the school, under the examination system it takes the form of prestige to the school and to the pupil, and (in the case of scholarships) a money payment to the latter. The examination system has the same bad effect on education as that produced by 'payment by results'. A historian of English education describes the effect of 'payment by results' as follows: 'The "results" procured were far too frequently mechanical results. It encouraged the neglect of the moral and other spiritual factors which constitute the most valuable parts of all education.'[1] He goes on to point out that the system restricted the field of education by causing schools to concentrate on 'profitable' subjects. Each of these charges can be brought against examinations. They procure

[1] Adamson, *Short History of Education*, pp. 307, 308.

'far too frequently mechanical results'. They encourage 'the neglect of the moral and other spiritual factors which constitute the most valuable parts of education'. 'Subjects can have meaning only as they are treated as aspects of active and living human experience. Whether, if considered from this point of view, they can continue to be examinable in the traditional manner is at least an open question.'[1] It is as impossible to examine in the most vital parts of education as to anatomize life on a dissecting table, and therefore the pressure of examinations continually pushes them into the background or out of sight. Further, it tends to restrict education to the subjects of the examination in question, with disastrous results in the case of examinations for university scholarships. I recently asked two mathematical scholars at Oxford who came from different schools how much time they had given during their last school year to other subjects than science and mathematics. In both cases the answer was 'one hour a week'. What an education: bad for the scholarship winners, but they at least had their reward; worse still for those whose education had been narrowed to win a scholarship and who failed to win one! I asked one of the latter class, who had tried unsuccessfully for a scholarship in science, what proportion of his time had been given to other subjects. The answer was 'six periods out of forty-two in the week'. It transpired that the only English literature read in the small time allotted to other subjects than his specialisation was Ibsen's *Ghosts*, a work presumably selected for its supposed connection with science, and considered to be English literature because it had been translated into English. Contrast with this miserable education the training given before the last war in the *Oberrealschule*, the

---

[1] Professor Kandel in *The Report of the Consultative Committee on Secondary Education*, p. 427.

secondary school in which the future scientists of Germany were educated, and in which less than half the time was allotted to science and mathematics: in the highest class eleven periods out of thirty-one were given to them, and the rest to other subjects.

Unfortunately there is a risk of the importance of examinations increasing. Already, when a boy's parents cannot afford to send him to a secondary school or a university, his whole life may depend on an examination result, and this is bad for him and for education. However disinterested he or his teacher may be, neither can forget what is at stake. As a boy of twelve I was a candidate for an Eton scholarship (which I failed to get), but my chief memories of the episode are of the roast mutton in College Hall and of eating strawberries in the playing fields. That is the right spirit in which to take an examination. My feelings at the time and my surviving memories would have been very different if my future had depended on getting a scholarship. But the number of people who will be able to take examinations in a light-hearted way seems likely to decrease.

We are moving from a society where men as a whole have been born to a certain condition of life and normally have accepted it, to a society, based as we hope on justice, where everyone will find the place to which his character and abilities entitle him. Well and good. But how easily such a society may become acutely competitive! Everyone must find his right place, everyone will desire to find it, and, unless human nature changes, will wish his place to be as high as possible. What possibilities of intense competition that suggests! And how will he find his place? How but by examination? And if so, education becomes a savage competitive system. It ceases to be education and becomes a road to a career. Shakespeare is read, not because he is Shakespeare, but because he is an examination subject in a syllabus, and the child who reads him sees behind the figures of Cordelia or Juliet or Hamlet or Lear the possibility of an examination question which may admit him to the university and determine the course of his life.

We should therefore adapt the wording of a historic motion in the House of Commons and resolve that the influence of examinations has increased, is increasing, and ought to be diminished, and in pursuance of this principle we should restrict their power and as far as possible use the school record and the interview as a substitute or part-substitute. It is impossible to get rid of them altogether; they are inevitable, I am afraid, for university scholarships and for primary university degrees, and in cases where a small selection has to be made out of a large number of candidates. Here we must endure what we must and minimise what we can. But it is difficult to see any conclusive reason why the most baneful of them, the G.E. Certificate, should exist. It does most damage, because it affects most children and distorts secondary education almost from the first. If we are told that some business men believe that a G.E. Certificate is better evidence of a child's capacities than its school record and its teacher's testimonial, we must reply that the education of thousands of children ought not to be spoilt each year for such a superstition. The G.E. Certificate had its uses when it was first instituted. It replaced a multitude of external examinations; the standard of teaching in some schools was low, and an external examination imposed on all schools was the best way of raising its level. To-day its work has been done; standards have been raised and established; and, under adequate inspection and with a prescribed curriculum, education may be allowed to replace the examination.[1] To say that without it the teacher cannot teach, and that the pupil will not learn, is to insult both and to ignore facts. Elementary and technical schools can do their work without the spur of an examination. Why should it be indispensable in secondary schools?

The second dragon in the path of true education is specialisation, which normally begins at sixteen. Life is more specialised than it was and more special knowledge is needed to live it competently. Further, limited specialisation after sixteen is educationally beneficial. But it has dangers, and it becomes disastrous when, in fact if not in theory, it excludes the wider human and spiritual interests, when these are ignored and slowly atrophied, when the pupil becomes a mere scientist or mathematician, a mere historian or modern linguist or classic. Then the adolescent suffers from the disease that so often attacks the man who is absorbed in his special occupation and becomes a mere industrialist, a mere economist, a mere civil servant, a mere grocer or artisan. Though there is plenty of materialism in England, the English are not fundamentally materialists. But the specialist tendency in education leads to materialism in effect, though not in intention. A boy takes to modern languages because they will be 'useful in after life', or to chemistry and physics because he intends to enter industry; or he must read the pre-registration subjects at school, so that he can start his full medical course at the university. Unless care is taken, the whole atmosphere of his education changes; the stress is on vocation, not on education; the liberal, human, spiritual element gives way to practical need and material advantage. The danger of specialisation varies with the subject. Some subjects imply, if they do not impart, a spiritual view of life; some subjects do not—or

[1] The Spens Report (pp. 254 f.) condemned it, but unfortunately failed to sentence it to death.

do so in a limited and inadequate way or to an infinitesimal
extent. Over-specialisation in mathematics and science is,
from this point of view, the more dangerous. It is indeed
deplorable if students in languages, literature and history
have no chance of at least keeping in touch with science
through their secondary school course. To know nothing
of science is to be, so far, intellectually maimed. But the
background of their studies is human conduct and human
ideals. What else is the subject of literature and history?
The subject of science is different; it deals with the material
world and the material aspects of man; the rest of him—
that is nine-tenths of him—is not its business. Over-
specialisation in it tends to produce scientists who are
admirable technicians but no more, and who therefore
lack the influence outside their subject, which its importance and the interest of the community demands.

Specialism is bad at school; it increases at the university.
If Professor Whitehead is right in saying that 'moral education is impossible without the habitual vision of greatness', then the moral education of most persons becomes
of little importance when they have obtained a G.E.
Certificate, and practically ceases when they reach the
University, where the student is absorbed in science or
economics or some other specialism, and is often unconscious that there is anything else in the world, just as in
later life and on a lower level some men are absorbed in
making money, equally unaware of other aims or interests.
But the quality of a civilisation does not depend only on
its science, economics or sociology but even more on its
standards, values, ideals, its sense of what is first-rate in life,
its religion. We act too often as if these, so far as education
is concerned, belong to a period that ends with the G.E.,
or at latest the Higher Certificate, and when these have
been passed, feel that we have done enough and can safely

settle down to the serious business of medicine or science
or economics or sociology.[1]

This disastrous practice has actually been erected into
a principle by Professor Dewy, whose influence on American education has been great and in some ways unfor-
tunate, and who urges 'the demarcation of secondary
work as the period of general training and culture, thus
making it the period of the knowledge of self in relation to
the larger meanings of life; and the reservation of the
higher institution for specific training, for gaining control
of the particular body of knowledge and methods of research
which fit the individual to apply truth to the guidance of
his own special calling in life'.[2] There speaks the voice of
an age concentrated on means and indifferent to ends.
Shrouded in the decent obscurity of Professor Dewey's
English, his theory may shock us less than if it was exposed
naked in plain language, but in effect it says: 'when your
secondary education ends, you can drop culture and the
"larger meanings of life": philosophy, history, literature
are done with (unless of course you are specialising in
them, when you will approach them as a "body of knowledge" for which special methods of research are required);
you will have solved their problems and penetrated their
mysteries; dismiss them and absorb yourself in your
profession.'

An admirable description of our practice, but how disastrous an ideal! As if there was any 'period' for 'the
knowledge of self in relation to the larger meanings of life';

[1] 'There is a considerable number of secondary schools in which the
subject (religious instruction) is not included in the time-table of the higher
Forms. In some of the latter religious instruction is discontinued in the Sixth
Form only; in others it is discontinued in the year in which the School
Certificate Examination is taken, or even earlier.' *Report of the Consultative
Committee on Secondary Education* (1938), p. 207.

[2] *Education To-day*, p. 52.

as if this knowledge could be more than begun in the 'secondary' stage of education! Say, if you believe it, that 'the larger meanings of life' are unimportant, but do not pretend that their study can be completed at school and therefore abandoned when we pass to the university.

It is to be hoped that we shall neither say the one nor pretend the other. It is indeed impossible and undesirable to abolish specialisation, but we can prevent it from becoming a cancer whose growth destroys studies essential to human beings as citizens and as men. Taking Professor Dewey's belief that the secondary stage in education is 'the period for the knowledge of self in relation to the larger meanings of life', we should revise it in the light of Plato's simpler and infinitely profounder words: 'The noblest of all studies is the study of what man is and of what life he should live.' We shall not agree with Professor Dewey that this 'noblest of all studies' can be completed in secondary education, but determine that, in some form or another, it is indispensable in every period of education from the nursery to the grave, and see that 'the higher institution' includes it, and is not entirely reserved for 'gaining control of the particular body of knowledge and methods of research which fit the individual to apply truth to the guidance of his own special calling in life'.

So far as I know, the only universities in Britain that make definite and deliberate provision for this are the Scottish, and these do so only partially and imperfectly. Philosophy in them must be taken by all students for the *pass* degree. But this does not apply to honours students, and philosophy is generously interpreted to include such subjects as economics, and in any case may be taken in the form of logic as well as moral philosophy and metaphysics. But those who read the two latter subjects are at least confronted in their university with 'the larger meanings of life' and 'the noblest of all studies'. Outside the Scottish universities no such provision exists; and the result in some cases is, as a professor in a new university famous for its work in applied science said to me, that 'we are turning out graduates who are barbarians'. That judgement may be too severe, but there is enough truth in it to merit attention.

The real remedy is a change of heart as much as a change of curriculum, a sense of our defects and their dangers. Plato wrote over the entrance of his Academy: 'Let no one enter who is ignorant of geometry.' An admirable motto, though it might exclude some otherwise deserving scholars! But perhaps at the moment we require a rather different one to inscribe over the doors of our schools and universities. I would suggest either the words from Plato quoted on the last page, or a choice from one of the two following sayings. 'By education I mean that training in excellence from youth upwards which makes a man passionately desire to be a perfect citizen, and teaches him how to rule, and to obey, with justice. This is the only education which deserves the name; the other sort of training, which aims at the acquisition of wealth or bodily strength, is not worthy to be called education at all.'[1] 'Whatever the world thinks, he who hath not much meditated upon God, the human mind, and the *Summum Bonum*, may possibly make a thriving earthworm, but will certainly make a sorry patriot and a sorry statesman.'[2]

[1] *Laws*, 643 f.
[2] Berkeley, *Siris*.

CHAPTER VI

EDUCATION FOR CITIZENSHIP

Greece is the mother of education for citizenship, as of so much else. Ancient Sparta devised the most complete and ruthless discipline ever conceived for turning men into citizens and soldiers, but Athens too had her more liberal methods of civic education, and though Pericles says that she did not rely on 'rigorous training' and 'state-made courage', he claims that his countrymen 'attend both to public and private duties and do not allow absorption in their own business to interfere with knowledge of the state's affairs'.[1] If we were asked what training in citizenship Britain gives, we might hesitate for an answer. In the last century, if the idea occurred to anyone, it interested very few: there is one reference to it in the index of an important book like Adams's *Evolution of Educational Theory* and none in Norwood's *English Tradition in England* or Nunn's *Education: its Data and First Principles*.[2] The foundation of the Association for Education in Citizenship in 1935 is perhaps the first sign of a general recognition, not only that there is such a subject but that it is very important.

Citizenship goes far beyond voting, paying taxes, sitting on a jury and the other duties expected by a nation from its members. Properly conceived, it involves all a man's actions which touch his fellow-citizens, and affect the

[1] Thucydides, II. 39, 40 (tr. Zimmern).

[2] Sir Percy Nunn's book however touches on the subject of citizenship without using the word (pp. 97–8) and the *Syllabuses in Use in the Demonstration Schools of London Day Training College* (1912) includes an admirable syllabus by him for teaching it.

health and well-being of the State; it is almost co-extensive with his duty to his neighbour. It includes everything which the law requires but also many duties about which it is silent and which are left to the individual conscience. It is not passive, not mere abstention from uncivic conduct. It is active. 'We regard the man who holds aloof from public duties not as "quiet" but as useless.'[1] 'Public life is a situation of power and energy; he trespasses against his duty who sleeps upon his watch as well as he that goes over to the enemy.'[2] The ideal state is one where every citizen is determined to be a part of the community, to share its burdens, to put its interest before his own, to sacrifice, if need be, his own wishes, convenience, time and money to it. It is a machine of which no part is idle or inefficient, none rusted, broken or ill-fitting, in which each pulley and cog takes up its full share of the load, and plays its part in the swift and smooth running of the whole. A man who evades his taxes is, so far, a bad citizen; but so is one who, in giving a vote for parliament, thinks only of his private interests, or is too indifferent or lazy to vote at all; so is the bad employer, whose treatment of his employees is not only a breach of the moral law, but adds to the social problems of the country; so are profiteers and the traders and clients of the 'black market'; so are workmen, who strike for some private interest when the existence of their country is at stake; so is the man who would be useful in local government but evades the burden, not because he cannot, but because he will not, spare the time.

There is plenty of bad citizenship in Britain, but there is probably more good citizenship here than in any other country, though it is not always labelled by that name. It

[1] Pericles (Thucydides, II, 40).
[2] Burke, *Thoughts on the Cause of the Present Discontents.*

appears in the numberless gifts and legacies for charitable and kindred objects, and in the uncounted instances where private effort performs duties of public interest, ranging from the Zoological Society to the care of the blind, from the Life-Boat Institution to the Scout Movement, from the preservation of scenery and historic buildings to the work of the Motoring Associations; look through the twenty-eight pages of Societies and Institutions in *Whitaker's Almanac* if you wish to see how many national activities depend on individual enterprise. There are idle rich in Britain, but they are fewer than the less conspicuous class of wealthy or well-to-do persons, who might live wholly selfish lives but who give time and money without stint to public service. A nation where all the universities have been created by private initiative, where municipal government and the administration of justice is largely carried on by unpaid work, where nearly half of the hospitals are managed and financed by private enterprise, where the Co-operative Movement was organised, where a third of the peace-time army is recruited by civilians giving up their leisure time to military training, where the Home Guard immediately created itself in response to public need, is not wanting in the spirit of good citizenship.

This spirit is the blood in a country's veins; where it is pure and flows strongly, national life will be healthy and vigorous, where it is thin or tainted, anaemia will be present and may pass into death. Important at any moment, it is most of all now, for we shall hardly survive the tensions of social change, certainly we shall not survive as a democracy, unless we have the community sense which will hold us together and enable us to move as a whole.

How can the spirit of citizenship be created or developed? How are good citizens made? This is part of the obscure and important question, where do men get their virtues? From what deep sources are drawn the courage and sacrifice shown in the air, by sea, on land? Where do the inhabitants of, for instance, Bermondsey or Bow, many of them living in intolerable surroundings, learn the qualities which enable them in peace to be decent, kindly people, and in war cheerfully to face the ruin of their homes and death from the air? How are such virtues to be preserved and extended? And, on the other hand, whence come our weaknesses and how shall we cure them—commercialism that sells beauty and debases standards for money, profiteering in every class and rank, partisanship and reckless statements in politics and outside it, the intellectual's betrayal of truth? Here are problems deserving inquiry more than many sociological studies, and very relevant to our future.

Citizens are made, not born; though men may be social animals, they are very apt to regard society as made for them, and as far as possible to use it for their own ends. It is an individual, not a member of a community, that issues from the womb, though these individuals have to live in the State and must learn how to do it. All human beings have the capacity to be citizens, but mere capacity is not enough; it needs developing and training. The vocational and personal sides of education will help little here. Men must learn how to earn their living; they must have the chance of developing body, mind and character to their full capacity. But earning a living and developing a personality are private matters, a concern of the individual; they will make a man a more useful member of the State but not necessarily a better citizen; they are no guarantee that he will serve it, study its interests, carry out his duties to it. Indeed if over-emphasised they may—and obviously often do—make him selfish and indifferent to the common good. Vocational and personal training are dangerously incomplete without the discipline which teaches men how to play their part in the State and makes them wish to do it. Education is a trinity, and one of its members is training in citizenship.

There are three elements in this training, of which the first and least important is teaching people the duties of a citizen and how to perform them. Mention education for citizenship, and the word 'civics' will probably rise into the mind; instruction on such subjects as 'the functions and institutions of government, both local and central, including Education, Public Health, Justice, Police, the Post Office, and the Defence Services, and the everyday work of local councils and of Parliament'.[1]

Eric Gill says in his *Autobiography*: 'The whole of my education was simply learning things out of little books and being able to remember enough to answer questions.' It is a common form of education. He continues: 'We are educated by the doing not by the learning and that is the whole secret of education, whether in schools or in workshops or in life.'[2] These warnings should be remembered in considering the teaching of citizenship. At school instruction of the kind proposed is apt to be little beyond 'learning things out of little books'; at that stage there is no opportunity for 'doing'. The subject has a specious attraction, and is sometimes described as up-to-date, realistic and related to the actual needs and life of the pupil. But though apparently practical, it is in fact purely academic. It consists almost entirely in imparting facts which have no relation to the actual life of the pupil, knowledge of which he can make no immediate use. The fact that he is being educated does not mean that he will

[1] *The Extra Year*, p. 114.
[2] Pp. 26, 28.

find the educational system of the country interesting; he takes no part in the work of local councils and of parliament; and if he does not happen to be criminal, he will have no first-hand experience of either justice or the police. Unless he has a retentive memory or lively imagination, the facts learnt will fall on his mind like dust, and, like dust, will in a few months or less be swept from it by succeeding impressions, leaving perhaps a few grains of knowledge behind. The clever pupil will retain more, but is likely to derive from his studies little beyond some up-to-date knowledge of facts, a vague plausibility about social questions, and a misleading belief that he understands them. For politics and government are essentially practical subjects, wearing very different faces in books and in life. Our views on them are of small value unless we have seen them at first-hand, and a schoolboy has not seen them at first-hand.

We must therefore not expect much from this form of instruction in citizenship. A certain amount of it is useful. In the hands of an inspired teacher, 'civics', like any other subject, can become a means of real education. But citizenship is better taught in a broader way and through the normal subjects of the school curriculum.[1] The most fruitful part of 'civics' in the narrower sense will probably be such things as visits to town councils, law-courts, parliament, factories, a slum, a distressed area, a housing estate, etc.—when possible, abroad as well as at home. This will not impart knowledge so much as strike the imagination by a glimpse into the real thing. It is not more than a glimpse; such visits show the outside rather than the

---

[1] There are valuable suggestions and discussions of the subject in *Education for Citizenship in Secondary Schools* (published under the auspices of the Association for Education in Citizenship); I do not agree with all its conclusions.

inside of problems, their existence, not their infinitely complicated conditions, but they leave in most minds a picture, a sense of real problems waiting to be solved such as all the 'little books' on civics will fail to give.

But, it will be said, the citizen needs more than that: he ought to know something about the machinery of government and the fabric of his civilisation, and at present we fail to give him this. Certainly: but school is not the time or place to give it. It should be given when it can be used, when men and women are citizens, with votes for parliament and local government, which cannot be given effectively without knowledge and, if given effectively, can change the conditions of their life. That is the time when the knowledge is needed, is welcomed—and is not available. 'We have been told', says the report quoted above, 'that in Senior Schools, it is the citizenship lesson in which the parents show most interest and themselves provide information and send up questions for answer.'[1] Those words indicate our neglected opportunity. Here are adults eager to learn about citizenship, unprovided with natural means to do so, and obtaining some knowledge indirectly through the lessons given to their children. But the senior school is not the best medium for teaching citizenship to men and women, nor have all adults access to it. What lovers of paradox we British are! Youth studies but cannot act; the adult must act, and has no opportunity of study; and we accept the divorce complacently. But action and thought, living and learning naturally belong together and should go hand in hand. Instruction in civics at school, if you will. But when the children are adults and have votes, let such instruction be available so that their votes can be used with intelligence. Our local government is not, in every city, the most successful of our institutions.

[1] *The Extra Year*, p. 115.

It might be improved if every elector had an opportunity of learning something about its nature and scope, and if perhaps the newly elected City or County Councillor, instead of being thrown headlong into his duties, to learn slowly what the sea is like by swimming in it, was given some instruction in the character and variety of this vast ocean; if, in fact, we did for our municipal rulers, as much as we do for an A.R.P. Warden; for local government is as complicated and important as fire-fighting. But this is a matter for Adult Education, hitherto so neglected in this country. At present we either fail to give our citizens the knowledge which citizens need, or push into the schools as much of it as we can manage, upsetting their curriculum and giving it at an age when it cannot be digested. We act like people who should try to give their children in a week all the food they require for a year; a method which might seem to save time and trouble, but would not improve digestion, efficiency or health. Some day, no doubt, we shall abandon this practice and give everyone a chance of thinking about life when he is facing it and about its problems when he has to solve them. When that day comes, we shall stop one of the chief sources of educational waste and inefficiency, and make the greatest advance in our history towards the creation of an educated democracy.

But even when 'civics' is taught and taught at the right age, our task is only beginning. Knowledge of political institutions, interest in social problems and current events will not of themselves make good citizens. Pascal says, 'How far it is from the knowledge to the love of God!' We may say, 'How far it is from civics to citizenship!' We must not make the error of Socrates and think that knowledge is virtue, or that duties are performed because they are known. To study the outlines of the government of the country, to visit city councils and law courts, to have an acquaintance with economics, public affairs and current events—all this barely touches the problem. Citizenship is not information or intellectual interest, though these are part of it; it is conduct not theory, action not knowledge, and a man may be familiar with the contents of every book on the social sciences without being a good citizen.

In citizenship, as in so many provinces in life, we provide means, teach their use, but give no sense of ends; tell people how to reach the goal but leave them ignorant and doubtful of the goal itself; like persons going on a holiday, who pack their clothes, collect journey money, food, golf clubs and tennis rackets, bring the car to the door or arrange transport to the station, and then discover that they have never decided where to go. That is impossible with holidays but common with life: and training for citizenship may include 'the Monarchy and what it stands for; the Houses of Parliament and their work, to include a short history; General Elections; the Public Services— the Army, Navy, Air Force, Police, Post Office, Ministry of Labour',[1] and much else, yet fail to give any vision of what the State should be.

Without such a vision, the knowledge may be misused or used blindly, the means wasted for lack of the right end. Not only so, but the chief impulse to action is lost. Here, as in every sphere of life, knowledge and intellectual equipment, without an ideal to drive them, are machinery without power, and there are few more melancholy or more common sights than admirable social machinery which cannot get up enough steam to work it. The sight of an inspiring goal gives the desire to reach it, and men devise means, when they are mastered by the passion for

[1] *The Extra Year*, p. 120f.

an end. Aristotle thought that God was the source of motion in the world, not by any direct intervention but by the response of human beings to the vision of himself. 'If God is always in that good state in which we sometimes are, this compels our admiration; and if in a better state, this compels it still more. And God *is* in a better state.... So he produces motion by the love he excites.... On this principle depend the heavens and the world of nature.'[1] Something of the sort is true of those visions of good which are called ideals. They have been the great sources of motion in the world, created its religious movements, made or helped its revolutions, and inspired its greatest men. Such visions 'compel our admiration and move us by the love they excite'.

This element, small in bulk, easily and quickly imparted, yet vast in importance, must not be overlooked and forms the second element in training for citizenship. People must have a vision of the ideal State, 'the holy City, new Jerusalem, coming down from God out of heaven', that they may know the goal of their quest and desire to reach it. A bible of citizenship might well be compiled containing the great visions of the meaning of the word. It would surely contain two passages which sum up the chief articles of the creed of citizenship—duty to country and (a more neglected obligation) duty to fellow citizens. The first extract is from the speech delivered by Pericles in 431 B.C. at the public funeral of the Athenians who had fallen in the Peloponnesian war:

Fix your eyes on the greatness of your country as you have it before you day by day, fall in love with her, and when you feel her great, remember that her greatness was won by men with courage, with knowledge of their duty, had with a sense of honour in action, who, even if they

[1] *Metaphysics*, 1072 b.

failed in some venture, would not think of depriving the country of their powers but laid them at her feet as their fairest offering.[1]

Anyone who has listened to addresses on patriotism or tried to compose one will realise the amount of thought as well as of feeling in these few words. Patriotism is 'falling in love' with one's country (the Greek word means passionate love), and love for a country, as for a human being, springs from some supreme attraction. Men fall in love with a country because of something great in it; this greatness was created by the courage and sense of duty and unlimited self-sacrifice of individual citizens, and it inspires others to these qualities and so is maintained and extended.

Another side of citizenship is stressed in the following passage in which it is defined as loving one's neighbour as oneself, and the State is regarded not as a mixed collection of individuals but as a united and affectionate family.

Do not the worst evils in a state arise from anything that tends to tear it asunder and destroy its unity; and is anything better than whatever tends to bind it together and make it one? Now a state is bound together by sharing joy and sorrow, by all its citizens being equally glad or grieved on the same occasion of gain or loss. The best ordered state will be one where the largest number of persons use the words 'mine' and 'not mine', 'another's' and 'not another's' in the same sense; it will most nearly resemble a single person. When we hurt a finger, the whole organisation of the body, unified under the ruling elements in the soul, feels it and shares the pain of the single member. The best organised community comes nearest that condition, recognises as part of itself the good and evil fortunes of each individual citizen, and shares as a

---

[1] Thucydides, II. 43. The word rendered 'powers' is the untranslatable ἀρεταί, a man's virtues, 'excellences', 'gifts' (see p. 99 f.).

whole in his joy or pain. In other states a man may regard one colleague as a friend in whom he has an interest, and another as a stranger with whom he has nothing in common. But that cannot happen with us. Our citizens must regard everyone he meets as brother or sister, father or mother, son or daughter, grandchild or grandparent. And a further point. Will you not expect them, not merely to use these family names, but to behave as a real family? In our state when things go ill or well with any of its members, everyone will use the word 'mine' in the same sense and say that all is well or ill with himself.[1]

Such ideals are part of a training in citizenship: they are an indication of the goal and an inspiration to reach it. But it is possible to see visions of goodness without following them, and knowledge of the right does not inevitably lead to right action. As Burke remarked:

Men are wise with but little reflection, and good with little self-denial, in the business of all times except their own. We are very uncorrupt and tolerably enlightened judges of the transactions of past ages; where no passions deceive, and where the whole train of circumstances, from the trifling cause to the tragical event, is set in an orderly series before us. Few are the partisans of departed tyranny; and to be a Whig on the business of an hundred years ago is very consistent with every advantage of present servility.... Many a stern republican, after gorging himself with a full feast of admiration on the Grecian commonwealths and of our true Saxon constitution, and discharging all the splendid bile of his virtuous indignation on King John and King James, sits down perfectly satisfied to the coarsest work and homeliest job of the day he lives in.

---

[1] Plato, *Republic*, 462 f. (tr. Cornford, slightly altered and shortened). Plato is speaking of the unity of feeling in his ruling class; but his words have a wider extension.

Bibles of citizenship—like other bibles—though guides to a better world, are not transport to one. That journey must be done by men on their own feet, though with direction from those who best know the road.

Here we come to the third and the most important element in training for citizenship, which we do not wholly neglect but provide sporadically and very incompletely. Citizenship, as I have urged, is practical not speculative, active not passive, an art not a theory—the art and virtue of living in a community. The good citizen, like the good soldier, has learnt to feel and act as a member of a body, to play his part in it, and, if need be, to sacrifice to it his interests and even his life, to do his duty to the State without compulsion and of his own free will. It is a difficult art, commoner perhaps in this country than in others, but not perfected, and needing to be learnt in every generation; a harmony of clashing forces—independence and respect for authority, individualism and team-work, self-assertion, self-discipline and self-sacrifice, initiative and subordination. Knowledge of 'civics' will help men to practise it, ideals will inspire and show the goal. But Whitehead's saying that moral education is impossible without the habitual vision of greatness needs to be completed by the remark of Aristotle that men acquire virtues, not by knowing what they are nor by talking about them nor by admiring and praising them but by practising them. We become punctual by continually being punctual, we acquire the habit of telling the truth by telling it; and we become good citizens by doing what good citizens do. Social virtue is learnt by social life. So its infant school is the family, where the members, living together, learn how to live together as members of a tiny community. The smaller the family, the worse the school.

But families exist in all countries. Where have the British

had the teaching which makes them not experts in the art but perhaps more expert than most peoples? I believe that much credit is due to religion. Foreigners recognise, even if we do not, the immense influence which Christianity has had on the national mind. Indeed, so far as we have a national mind at all, it has been mainly made by Christianity. For many hundred years most of the population of these islands heard its message preached. The conception of the Fatherhood of God, leads logically to the Brotherhood of Man; texts like 'Ye are members one of another' imply no doubt a wider citizenship than anything on earth, but they imply citizenship and enforce a sense of community. Men cannot listen to such words Sunday after Sunday without some trace of them remaining, even if it is only an ideal in the background of the mind, a pricking of the conscience, a call to the deeper side of their nature. Then too the nation has learnt much, painfully and with many failures, in a thousand years of history. It must have learnt something when Roman Catholics, Anglicans and Puritans managed to be loyal Englishmen in the days of Queen Elizabeth: more in the bitter struggles between 1640 and 1660: most of all perhaps in the admirable school of parliamentary government, where men learn to fight without becoming enemies, to lose without resentment and to win without pushing victory too far, and where the verdict of a majority is accepted but the rights of the minority are not forgotten. These are among the schools where the English have had a general social education. But there are several institutions which give it in a specific form, institutions whose members learn the habit of citizenship by being citizens. The Scout and Guide Movement, the Boys' and Church Lads' Brigades, Boys' and Girls' Clubs, are among them. Another great school of citizenship in England is the Trade

Union, where several millions of Englishmen learn to subordinate private wishes and opinions to a common policy, and a mass of individuals becomes a disciplined army. A strike may be inconvenient or even unjustifiable, but men who will throw up their work and livelihood for a common cause, possibly against their desire or even their judgement, have learnt one at least of the lessons of social education—how to act as a community.

But the greatest instrument of social education in England affects a different and much smaller though very important class. It is the so-called public school, which should rather be called the residential school. Whatever its weaknesses, it has by its very nature one great virtue. It is an incomparable school of social education, of citizenship, where boys learn citizenship by being citizens. That is what a public school boy is—a citizen. He has two countries—his school, a community of perhaps 600 boys, and his house, a community of some 50 boys. He is a member, a citizen of both these communities, and in each of them has his place and privileges and duties. He lives inside them for eight months of the year. Their problems, their interests, their happenings are before his mind on every day of those eight months. Never in later life will he be so intensely a member of a community, never again will he live so completely in and for a community, as he does in these school years. Living thus as a citizen he imbibes instinctively the fundamental principles of good citizenship. To feel yourself part of a community which you have a share and a responsibility in making, whose successes are somehow your successes and whose failures cast their shadow on you, to be able to obey and to live and co-operate with other members of the community, this is the essence of citizenship, and this the boy at a good residential school learns unconsciously

every day of his life, not by being taught it, but by practising it. The state no doubt is small, but there is good hope
that this habit of acting as a member of a community may
become part of his nature and survive when he finds
himself in that larger theatre which is called a country
and that still larger one which is called the world. Schools
and trade unions may be narrowed to serve the interests
or represent the views of a class. But this is not inherent
in their nature, nor do these incidental weaknesses alter
the fact that they create a spirit which may serve wider
uses.

But the residential school does not provide for the masses
of the nation, or for those boys who either cannot gain
admission to it or whose parents prefer the day school.
Where will they learn the virtues of the citizen by living
as citizens?

One means is the nursery school. Plato thought that
the State should educate children 'before they can understand language and are therefore incapable of appre-
ciating any sort of instruction'; for the first 'three years
are a considerable part of life to be passed ill or well'.[1]
The nursery school is based on this idea though it takes
children a little later and, while the character is as little
set as the body, trains them by the mere attendance at
school in the art of living in a community. Nursery
schools, like all institutions, have dangers but there is no
reason why they should impair family life and responsibility; they supply something which the small family
cannot give, and they can do much to correct the disastrous influence of bad homes.

In the next stages the elementary school can be organised
to give a practical training in citizenship, in so far as the
teaching, interests and life of the school can centre in its

[1] *Laws*, 791 f.

neighbourhood. 'To be attached to the subdivision, to love the little platoon we belong to in society, is the first principle (the germ, as it were) of public affections' (Burke). At a later age the secondary day school can develop community life through school games, societies, camps and journeys abroad, etc. Here the British day school does far more for its pupils than similar institutions abroad, which limit education to the class room and consider their work done when lessons end. It is an unrecognised debt due to the residential school, from which the day school has learnt the value of extra-curricular activities, adapting them to its different circumstances. But whereas such activities are spontaneous and inevitable in the residential school, they could only be organised in the day school by the care, ingenuity and self-sacrifice of the staff, and they are one of the splendid things in British education. The good day school does everything in this direction which circumstances allow; but it can claim far less of a boy's time and life than a residential school and he is far less a citizen of it. Its weakness on this side can be seen in the newer universities, which, themselves mainly non-residential and drawing their students chiefly from non-residential schools, have in general little corporate spirit or corporate loyalty. They have done a great work in the country which must rely on them for a large part of its future leaders, but they teach rather than educate.

The following extract from *The Times* of 29 November 1937, reveals a melancholy lack of spirit of citizenship in a highly educated class of the community:

Disappointment at the response to the —— University's Extension Fund Appeal was expressed at the annual meeting of the Court of Governors to-day. The Vice-Chancellor said that 2800 copies of the Appeal had been sent to old students and only 79 had replied. It had been suggested, he continued, that old students should subscribe £1 a year for seven years, which was not an excessive amount, as most old students owed their present positions to the education they received at the university. The poor response might be partly due to the fact that students at provincial universities had become too much accustomed to receiving everything for nothing.

It is certainly surprising that, though the graduates of the university concerned had been mainly educated at public expense and largely owed their income and position to the university, there should have been so much lower a percentage of gratitude among them than among the ten lepers in the New Testament, of whom one expressed thanks for being healed. Whether such a spirit is common in other universities, I do not know.[1]

Whatever has been done, much remains to do. The only thorough provision, in our educational system, for training in citizenship is in the residential school—and that is unintentional. For the rest, however much the day school does, its conditions do not allow it to do as much as the nation needs, and in any case the mass of the population at present leave school at fourteen and in the future will leave it at fifteen or sixteen—ages at which training for citizenship is quite incomplete. What can we do?

The development of school camps will help; the Youth Movement has great possibilities. Still more will be done if some form of conscription or of national service persists after the war. It may take the shape of compulsory labour camps, which all members of the community must attend. They could give to the nation the training in community life which the residential school now gives to a few. They

---

[1] For an informed criticism of the newer universities see *The Universities in Transformation*, by A. Löwe (an important book) and *Blind Guides*, by D. M. Paton.

would make every Englishman 'work at least once with his hands and thus contribute towards the building up of his people. Above all, we want those who are in sedentary occupations to experience what manual labour is, so that they may feel understanding and sympathy for those of their countrymen whose lives are spent in the fields, the factory or the workshop. We want to abolish for ever that attitude of superiority which unfortunately so many of our intellectuals adopt towards the manual workers,[1] and we wish them to realise that they too will be worth all the more if they know themselves to possess a capacity for physical work. But the ultimate aim behind labour service is to promote mutual understanding between the different classes, and thus strengthen the spirit of national solidarity among the whole people.' These are Hitler's words. But the fact that Hitler spoke them does not lessen their wisdom.

Our first task is to realise that the spirit of citizenship does not grow into a strong plant without cultivation; our problem will be solved when everyone born in Britain has the knowledge needed by a citizen, has seen the vision of what citizenship is, and has been trained in it by living with others, not merely as an individual, but as a member of a community whose life and responsibilities he shares. I have put these three requirements in inverse order. The most important is the last.

---

[1] I doubt if this is true of English 'intellectuals'.